Relationship and
Leadership Strategies

Relationship and
Leadership Strategies

*Commonsense Ideas on How to
Get Along Better with the
Important People in Your Life*

Paul E. Heacock

Order this book online at www.trafford.com
or email orders@trafford.com

Most Trafford titles are also available at major online book retailers.

Printed in the United States of America.

ISBN: 978-1-4907-3019-6 (sc)
ISBN: 978-1-4907-3021-9 (e)

Library of Congress Control Number: 2014905013

Heacock, Paul 1945–
BASIC Relationship and Leadership Strategies/Paul E. Heacock p. cm.

Trafford rev. 06/20/2014

 www.trafford.com

North America & international
toll-free: 1 888 232 4444 (USA & Canada)
fax: 812 355 4082

Especially for Abby, my favorite (and only) grandchild. May you discover and value these BASIC strategies and commonsense principles earlier and apply them more consistently than I have.

Abby, keep in mind the following quote from George Bernard Shaw that you asked me to put in the book just for you:
Life isn't about finding yourself. Life is about creating yourself.

With appreciation to all the people I worked with at General American Life Insurance Company, Frankona America Reinsurance Companies, Human Dynamics, and MutualAid eXchange.

Also for all the people I have interacted with over the years that have helped me think through these ideas. With special thanks to Bob Dinkins, Bob Gibson, Jon Heacock, Janet Horner, Dale Hotze, Bill and Paula Kay, Cary Phillips, Jim Temme, Danny Walker, Dave Wine, and Dan Wolgemuth.

Contents

Guiding Wisdom

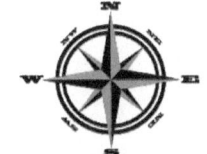

The greatest truths are too important to be new.
—Somerset Maugham

Real human freedom is the ability to pause
between the events of our lives and choose how we will respond.
—Rollo May

What gets rewarded is what gets done.
—Dr. Michael LeBoeuf

What is necessary to change a person is to
change his awareness of himself.
—Abraham Maslow

Yesterday is a cancelled check, tomorrow is a promissory
note, today is the only cash you have, so spend it wisely.
—Kay Lyons

I have been through some terrible things in my
life, some of which actually happened.
—Mark Twain

Urgent things are seldom important, and
important things are seldom urgent.
—Charles Hummel

In times of rapid change, experience could be your worst enemy.
—J. Paul Getty

Every actor needs a different director at different
times; it is my job to be that director.
—Steven Spielberg

Our frame of reference gives words meaning.
—Unknown

People don't care how much you know until
they know how much you care.
—Teddy Roosevelt

When the student is ready, the teacher arrives.
—Buddhist Proverb

The average person has a lot of common sense
because they haven't used any of it yet.
—Charley Jarvis

Everything should be explained as simply as possible, but no simpler.
—Albert Einstein

Foreword by an Old Friend

Forty-five years—not a long time in the history of modern business, but long enough to have witnessed firsthand the evolution of one of the most well-balanced and best leaders I have ever known—Paul Heacock.

Paul and I began our professional careers together at General American Life Insurance Company in St. Louis as accountants. Actually, we were junior accountants since he didn't have his bachelor's degree at that time and my degree was in general business, not accounting. We mastered the technical side of insurance accounting rather quickly. Then we moved on to lead the very accounting departments that wouldn't hire either of us as anything but apprentices.

Even as our careers took us in different directions, we must have made the transition to leadership effectively, having both risen to senior executive positions in multinational companies and owning and operating our own successful businesses. Our success was not because of any technical knowledge we had developed, but because of the leadership and people skills we learned and applied along the way.

We learned a lot from each other in those forty-five years. I think I got the better end of the deal, watching and learning from one of the best. He says I have changed over the years (I think he means for the better), but he has always been the same calm, patient, caring leader, the equal of which I seldom see.

Though we have individually moved many times, I am so happy our paths have come full circle, and Paul and I are both in Kansas City as we begin retirement (that means no longer working for a paycheck). While we plan to stay busy with selected projects and raising grandchildren, we will have even more opportunities to use the *BASIC Leadership and Relationship Strategies*.

Enjoy the read.

If you're young, applying these concepts can immediately better your life and relationships.

If you are in the middle of your working life, application of these ideas will make the remainder of your career and relationships more fulfilling.

Even if you're "mature" like Paul and me, applying these great ideas to your relationships will significantly enhance the golden years.

Dale Hotze
Friend

Foreword by a New Colleague

I first met Paul Heacock during a company luncheon, right after I delivered the first segment of a mindfulness workshop that he references later in the book. He approached me in an unassuming, honest, and straightforward manner and said, "You're not teaching anything new here." I paused to contemplate whether he was a satisfied or dissatisfied customer and then decided to practice what I had just preached. "You're right," I said. Then with comedic timing, he returned with, "We just need to be reminded." I bonded with Paul in that moment, which may be why he shared his BASIC principles with me at that time. I was surprised, excited, and impressed. We were both advocating the same things, only he managed to do so without a psychology degree!

Okay, I guess it's time to confess that I'm a college professor. Overgeneralizing (though not by much), we worry about the layperson's approach to "truth." While we know we're not the only well-read individuals in the world, we do believe we're one of the few who *empirically test* what we read. We sigh when we hear people say things like "Psychology is the study of the things we already know using language we don't understand." Sometimes what we already know is wrong and needs to be re-viewed (and I mean "view it again" by that). The fact that Paul had a segment about this in his book reinforced that I was speaking to a peer: "Call on past experiences, but assess each circumstance anew." Yes!

At a Global Well-being Conference in 2010, Jim Clifton (chairman and CEO of Gallup) led a group of professionals and professors through a "what-if" exercise: "Wouldn't it be great if practice and research, if business leaders and professors, got together to talk? Wouldn't it be great if we put value on the critical work that each side brings to the table?" He complimented the faculty in attendance for being "good groundbreakers," then he praised the businesspeople for being "town fathers and town mothers who lead the way to change." Mr. Clifton challenged us to share conversations during the conference. "Create interventions that raise global well-being. Every leadership position counts." I was there and took note because I yearned for that kind of collaboration. It took four years to occur.

When he gave me a copy of his manuscript, Paul asked for permission to quote something from my workshop. I felt honored to be included among the many professionals he valued. This book is an accurate synthesis of a treasure chest of scholarly work. It is written in an honest and conversational style. It is the product of significant insight.

Paul Heacock is, indeed, a town father who *will* raise global well-being.

Maria Hunt, PhD
Professor of Psychology
Avila University

Preface

This book incorporates the leadership and personal relationship lessons I have learned as

- a business leader since 1967;
- a marriage partner since 1967;
- a parent of two very special children—Missy, our "severely handicapped" daughter (born in 1969), and Jennifer (born in 1973), our "normal" daughter;
- a grandparent of Abigail (born in 2002).

In the Beginning

I was born in St. Louis, Missouri, in 1945.

I am told I was an observant child—often getting me and sometimes my brother, Jon Wayne Heacock (two years younger and on the right in this picture), in trouble. My mother loved to tell about the doctor being concerned that Jon was not gaining as much weight as he should in his first year. Mom and Dad also noticed I was gaining quite a bit of weight. One day, the mystery was solved when Dad caught me "ambushing" Jon, stealing and drinking his bottle. Sorry, Jon.

Speaking of Dad, my father, Benjamin Franklin Heacock, was an important role model for me when I was growing up. Dad was born into a very poor family in Southeast Missouri. He left school in the second grade and thus was never able to read. He married Mom when they were both very young. Although he loved the rural countryside where he grew up, he moved to the big city of St. Louis and worked in a manufacturing job most of his adult life. He died in 1990 from mesothelioma that he contracted while working in that shingle factory.

Dad's inability to read first became apparent to me when he was temporarily laid off from his job and had to file for unemployment insurance. Every week, either Jon or I had to fill out the unemployment forms for him. Although he could not read, he was a very proud man and had mostly sheltered us from this disability up to that point in time. I remember watching this hardworking, proud man humble himself to accept that he was incapable by himself of filling out the forms to get some needed temporary financial assistance for the family.

This was a profound moment in my life—one of the first times I remember understanding how important it is to love and trust and build relationships with the people in your life. Despite all the challenges he faced in his life, I never once heard him speak badly about anyone. I wish I could say the same about myself.

By the way, you may have noticed that my dad's full name is *Benjamin Franklin* Heacock. My brother's full name is *Jon Wayne* Heacock, which caused me many times to wonder who Paul Eugene was! Maybe that will be the subject of my next book.

While growing up in North St. Louis and attending Baden Elementary and Beaumont High School, I had many part-time jobs that further opened my eyes to the importance and positive power of good relationships with the people who come in and out of our lives. Some examples of my experiences include the following:

- Shined shoes in the local tavern (where my customers, for obvious reasons, often could not evaluate the quality of my work).
- Purchased and resold farm fresh eggs door to door.
- Manually set bowling pins for ten cents a game at the Baden Lanes (just before they converted to the new fancy automatic pin setters).
- Started an integrated *St. Louis Globe-Democrat* paper route, with my good friend Johnny Clark, serving our segregated neighborhoods.
- Raised and sold parakeets.

- Created and self-published a weekly neighborhood newspaper (the *Baden Evening World*) with Jon.
- Lived behind and worked in my family's many grocery stores.
- Fried hamburgers and made milk shakes in the Dairy Dell, a local fast-food restaurant.
- Worked a summer job at the U.S. Post Office.

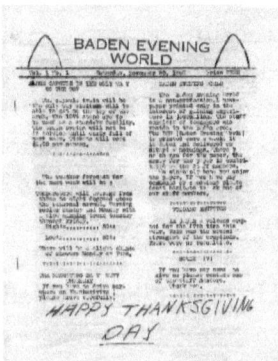

When I graduated from Beaumont High School in 1964, I decided that I had enough of school and would get a real job. My uncle was a member of the United Steelworkers union and helped me get a second-shift job at the American Can Company. The pay was great ($3 an hour!), and I was on my own with lots of my own spending money.

Two weeks later, I realized I had made a big mistake. I quickly enrolled for the January 1965 semester at Florissant Valley Community College with an even greater appreciation for education and learning. Working in a union environment was a unique lesson on maximizing my ability to get along positively with other people. For example, I started coming to work a little early to prefill some labels to make my job a little easier once the workday started. I quickly found out this working off the clock did not sit well with my fellow union members. I stopped coming in early.

There was one big advantage, however, to working at the can company between the end of high school in June of 1964 and starting my junior college adventure in January 1965. I earned a significant amount of money, and with the savings I had from all my other part-time jobs, I was able to purchase a new 1964 Chevy Impala Super Sport. One night around midnight, after working the second shift, I went to my car and opened the door. I looked in and knew something was wrong, but I could not figure out what was not right—until I started to sit down. Someone had stolen the bucket seats! I had a bowling ball in the trunk and had to sit on the bowling ball to drive the car home. Driving a car while sitting on a bowling ball is quite difficult but also a good lesson in dealing with whatever life brings.

I made a relatively successful transition from a steelworker to junior college student. I must admit, though, that one of the most expensive lessons I learned at Florissant Valley was the card game Hearts. I graduated with an associate certificate in finance and accounting in June of 1967. I was even elected to the school's hall of fame, much to the astonishment and humor of many of my high school and college pals (fellow members of the International Brotherhood of Gluttons—perhaps the subject of a third book). I have photographic proof of my election, but the hall of fame has apparently moved. No one can find it now. But I know it is there. Somewhere.

In 1966, I met a young lady named Janis Hertrich. She was dating one of my best friends at the time. To make a long story shorter, Janis and Keith broke up, and Janis and I became a couple. So much so that we got engaged in November 1966 and decided to get married in June 1967. One of her conditions for our marriage was that I would find a full-time professional job and finish my college education at St. Louis University's night school.

In June 1967, two weeks before we were married, I started my professional career as a junior accountant with General American Life Insurance Company in St. Louis. Paul Laut gave me this first opportunity to work in an office environment. I will always be grateful for him "taking a chance on me." Paul was a skilled accountant and taught me a lot about insurance accounting and the business of insurance. This job eventually evolved into my first supervisory experience and introduced me to John Biggs, who became my mentor. I learned a lot about the insurance business and about relating with others from watching and working with Mr. Biggs. It was also in this job that I met my lifelong friend and colleague Dale Hotze, whose guidance and counsel (what we called driveway talks) has been invaluable for both of us over the years.

I am proud to say that with lots of help and support from Janis, I was

able to graduate from St. Louis University with a bachelor's degree in accounting and finance in 1971. I was the first person in my extended family to attend, much less graduate, college.

In 1969, our first daughter, Melissa Ann, was born. At ten days old, Missy suffered a brain aneurysm. Her two doctors said she would not live another ten days. However, she lived in our home twenty-nine plus years, outliving both doctors. The aneurysm did lead to hydrocephalus (water on the brain). A cerebral shunt was placed in Missy's skull to drain the excess fluid into other body cavities from where it could be resorbed. We (mostly Janis) had to pump the shunt manually several times a day to make it do its work. While the shunt saved her life, the hydrocephalus did cause damage that ultimately limited Missy's physical and mental development. Subsequent testing defined Missy's development as less than that of a normal six-month-old child. While Missy never spoke a word, she taught Janis and me so much about life, much of which I've incorporated into these writings. The most powerful lessons are to appreciate every day, cherish what you have, and do not worry about what you don't have.

In 1973, we were blessed with our "normal" daughter, Jennifer Jean. Jennifer, in her own special way, has offered additional life lessons. I often tease Jennifer about the night she went to sleep as Cinderella and woke up as Godzilla. An exaggeration, no doubt, but the statement also includes more than a grain of truth.

In 1979, I accepted a new job and moved my wife (the only child) and our two daughters "256.6 miles west of Grandma's driveway" to the Kansas City area. I became the first controller of the newly formed Frankona America Life Reassurance Company. This is important to my journey because Frankona was based in Munich, Germany, and provided very generous (European-style) benefits. They offered more vacation time than I could ever use since it was very difficult to find respite care for Missy. So I had some downtime that would soon be taken up by what was to become a lifelong passion for me.

The concepts and ideas for this book had been bubbling around in my mind since early childhood but really began to crystallize in the late '80s. I was approached by a national seminar company to coauthor a course intended to help technical people (programmers, tradesmen, actuaries, lawyers, accountants, etc.) better make the transition from their technical job responsibilities to a leadership role. Who or what are technical people, you might ask. Here is a hint: "These are the voyages of the Starship Enterprise." Yes, Mr. Spock and Data are movie and television examples of technical people. Neither Spock nor Data can understand why their captain would personally want to beam down and lead the team to the all-female planet they had just discovered. From the perspective of these technical people, it is not logical!

As mentioned above, I had some excess vacation time, and I jumped at the opportunity to work with the national seminar company. As part of this course development process, I was given unlimited access to the seminar company's resource library and allowed to attend any seminar they offered, free of charge. The late '80s was well before the Internet, Google, and Wikipedia. In those now seemingly ancient times, the best sources of data on any business subject, including relationship and leadership strategies, were printed books and the hot new technology of the day—audio cassette tapes. The audio cassette tapes were a great source of information but relatively expensive. Working with this national seminar company gave me access to a wealth of materials that I otherwise would never have been able to study.

About this same time, I also reconnected with one of my childhood friends, Jim Temme. Jim and I grew up together in Baden and played baseball most of our youthful summers. Jim, after a successful management career with the American Cancer Society, became a very prominent full-time professional speaker and writer. Jim inspired me and encouraged me to pursue speaking and writing as my time allowed.

My basement is still full of audio cassette tapes I found especially enlightening. Due to my arrangement with the national seminar company, I was able to purchase the cassette tapes at a significant discount. I also attended many live seminars offered in the Kansas City area. While developing the leadership skills for technical people course, I began to realize that most of what was being included in this course and in all the other courses I audited or reviewed was built around common (or what I eventually came to call BASIC) concepts. It seemed that no matter what the subject was, much of the most essential content was similar, often just rephrased or repackaged. I was able to identify about twenty BASIC themes that covered 80 percent or so of the other course content. Even more importantly, I also came to realize that most of these general business themes, in addition to addressing leadership issues, also applied to my other roles in life as a marriage partner and as a parent.

More recently, I have been working with my friend and colleague Cary Phillips to flesh out more of these BASIC strategies. Cary and I first met when I was teaching business and financial literacy courses for Employers Reinsurance Company (now part of Swiss Re). He now facilitates this same business literacy course in addition to working with me on leadership training. Cary has encouraged me to write this book. I have learned a lot from him and appreciate and recognize his contributions to my personal growth.

The good news in all this is that many of us already know most of these concepts. The challenge is to pause and remember them when we need them. To use something effectively, it must be at our conscious level. To be at our conscious level, we must practice it. Like me, you probably can recall many instances when you did some things as a leader, partner, or parent and then quickly realized you knew better. Somerset Maugham is credited by some sources for having once said,

> The difference between mediocrity and success
> is often the difference between common
> knowledge and application of same.

I believe most of us, when we reach adulthood, have and continually develop a BASIC tool kit for dealing with life. The key to being more successful or the best we can be lies not in learning a whole bunch of new things but rather in learning how to apply and rely on what we already know (in many ways our common sense). One of the main purposes of this book is to help you refresh and expand that tool kit. Better relationships are about tools, options, choices, freedom, and being in control of yourself.

- The more *tools* you have, the more *options* you have.
- The more *options* you have, the more *choices* you have.
- The more *choices* you have, the more *freedom* you have.
- The more *freedom* you have, the more you are in *control*.

Another key to best benefiting from this book is to open up your thought process and let some new or refreshed ideas in for review. For the "creatively challenged," I suggest Roger von Oech's book *A Whack on the Side of the Head*. In his book, Mr. von Oech discusses hard and soft thinking. We need to do both hard thinking and soft thinking. Hard thinking is that rational thinking we all need to do before we seriously plan or take certain actions. Hard thinking provides a needed reality check. Soft thinking, on the other hand, is the key to creativity. It is the "what-if" process. Soft thinking is often the key to finding new and better ways to accomplish things. As you consider the various topics and suggestions in this book, try to avoid statements like "That will never work in my situation" or "I've tried that before" or "He doesn't know my boss or spouse or kids." Rather, stay open, let some new or refreshed ideas in, mull them around, and then apply the necessary reality checks.

Use the BASIC strategies suggested in this book to get into that toolbox, dust off some of those tools, and maybe find a few new tools (not necessarily better tools, just new tools). You will also find new ways to use some of the tools you already have.

Remember, the main purpose of the BASIC strategies is to help you expand your tool kit. As Abraham Maslow once said,

> If you only have a hammer, you tend to
> see every problem as a nail.

I've seen this quote paraphrased as follows:

> If the only tool you have is a hammer, the
> whole world begins to look like a nail.

The key is to learn to pause, open up your thinking and reaction process, and let in some new or refreshed ideas for review. This process will allow you to expand the options/freedom you have to better relate with the most important people in your life, in the roles you may play in life—leader, partner, and parent.

This book represents my conclusions from reviewing hundreds of audiotapes, books, and seminars on leadership and personal relationships.

The BASIC Acronym

O ne day while I was on my daily walk, listening to my audiotapes, I began to think of an acronym to represent these common concepts. Over the next few months, I came up with the acronym of BASIC, composed of the following:

- *B* (there are two *B*s)—understanding *behavior* and keeping a *balance* in our personal and professional lives.
- *A* is for begin each circumstance *anew*.
- *S* means be *situational*.
- *I* stands for watch the *I*.
- *C* (there are three *C*s)—improve *communication*, handle people with *care*, and use your *common sense*.

As illustrated above, the bottom building blocks represent the need for a solid foundation based on the three *C*s: communication, care, and common sense. The top blocks illustrate the primary need to understand some high-level truths about human behavior and the absolute significance of having a proper balance in our lives. The middle blocks are where flexibility is needed when applying the BASIC strategies by assessing each circumstance anew, being situational, and staying properly mindful of our own abilities and shortcomings by watching the *I*.

The ultimate value of the BASIC strategy revolves around how we use this knowledge in a given situation. If we know all the theory but are unable to apply it at the right time—so what! We must keep these commonsense tools prominent in our thought process. Ideally, the BASIC acronym will help keep these strategies in the forefront of your mind.

This book presents a BASIC approach to improved success in our professional and personal lives, specifically in our roles as leader, partner, or parent. These are some common thoughts of a common man based on proven leadership and relationship theories tempered with some common sense.

An Important Personal Disclaimer

M any times I have listened to a speaker, or especially a politician, and wondered, is that person real? Are they really that good? Can their life be that perfect? Experience has taught me that we are all human, and we all make mistakes and fail at times. As my friend Cary Phillips often says, "Life is hard, get a helmet."

One very important disclaimer. I want to make it very clear that *I do not consider myself to be the perfect leader, partner, or parent!* There are many people in my life who could tell you stories of me failing in each of my roles. I could make a long list of messes I've made, of people I have unintentionally hurt. However, what I do know is that when I remember and use the concepts discussed in this book, I am much better—a much better leader, a much better partner, a much better parent, and yes, even a much better grandparent.

Summary of the BASIC Strategy—Page 1

BASIC Relationship and Leadership Strategies

"Real human freedom is the ability to pause between the events of our lives and choose how we will respond." - Rollo May

Understand **B**ehavior and keep your **B**alance

Begin each circumstance **A**new

Be **S**ituational

Watch the "**I**"

Practice **C**ommunication, **C**are and **C**ommon sense

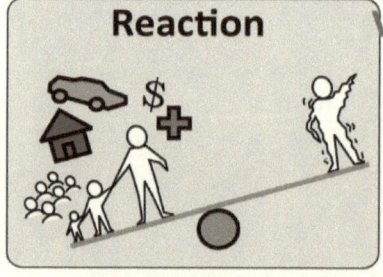

Reaction

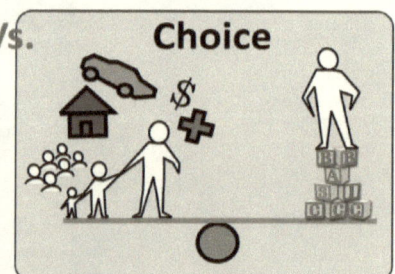

Vs. Choice

"The greatest truths are too important to be new." - Somerset Maugham

BASIC Relationship and Leadership Strategies

11100 W. 124th Street • Overland Park, KS 66213
913-707-7079 • www.basicrelationships.com
For more information, email Paul Heacock at pheacock@kc.rr.com

Copyright © Basic Relationships 2014
V 2.0

Summary of the BASIC Strategy—Page 2

Understand Behavior

- Abandon any hope of ongoing control over how others act
- People make conscious decisions about their behavior
- The only way to get the best of an argument is to avoid it
- What gets rewarded is what gets done
- Model the behavior you desire
- 80/10/10 rule

Be Situational

- "Every actor needs a different director at different times, it is my job to be that director." - Steven Spielberg
- Be the senior partner in a relationship
- Values and significant emotional events impact behavior
- Different frames of reference cause different reactions
- There are no absolutes - flexibility is a sign of maturity
- People often need your care most when they deserve it the least

Improve Communication

- Practice effective listening - must be learned and consciously activated
- Pick your words carefully
- Remember all of us are imperfect communicators - but some are farther from perfection than others

Keep Balance In Your Personal Life

- Our chosen reaction causes stress - not events and circumstances
- Live in the present
- Keep your perspective
- Seek and use humor for energy

Keep Balance In Your Professional Life

- Balance interpersonal and technical skills (85/15 rule)
- Beware of tyranny of the urgent
- Don't confuse activity with results
- Don't be a wandering generality

Handle People With Care

- We get back from people what we give them
- People don't care how much you know until they know how much you care
- When the student is ready, the teacher arrives
- Be tough on results but tender on people
- Attack the problem, not the person

Begin Each Circumstance Anew

- Call on past experiences but assess each circumstance anew
- Avoid stereotyping
- Watch for preconceived negative biases
- Make the essential transition to leadership
- Parents as leaders

"The BASIC truths are too important to be new."
- Paul Heacock

Watch the "I"

- Build a strong positive self image
- There is no "I" in teamwork
- Build relationships - network (85/15 rule)
- Embrace the big picture
- Recognize political and power forces
- Delegate at work & home

Use Your Common Sense

- If all else fails - trust your common sense
- Listen to your intuition
- Watch for BFOs (*Blinding Flashes of the Obvious*)
- Knowledge without common sense is folly
- "The average person has an enormous reservoir of common sense because they haven't used any of it yet." - Charlie Jarvis

Relationship and Leadership Strategies

11100 W. 124th Street • Overland Park, KS 66213
913-707-7079 • www.basicrelationships.com
For more information, email Paul Heacock at pheacock@kc.rr.com

Copyright © Basic Relationships 2014
V.2.1-052814

Understand Behavior

There are two *B*s in the BASIC strategy. The first *B* is to understand behavior. In other words, to understand better what makes people act the way they do.

Understand behavior key concepts:

- Abandon any hope of ongoing control over how others act.
- People make conscious decisions about their behavior.
- The only way to get the best of an argument is to avoid it.
- What gets rewarded is what gets done.
- Model the behavior you desire.
- The 80/10/10 rule.

Abandon Any Hope of Ongoing Control over How Others Act

I submit that those of you with children may have already abandoned any such hope, at least in the short run. Yes, you can make people do things your way in the short run while you are around. However, it is much more productive in the long run if you get others to do what you want because they want the same things. Think of the difference between desire and compliance. In other words, *want to* is much better and longer lasting than *have to*. We must teach others to make the best decisions on their own. Here is a shocking thought: *When your children make the most important decisions of their lives, chances are you will not be there!* I cannot think of a more powerful way to emphasize how important it is to set the right tone so that others want to do the right thing. You cannot rely on being there to make them do so.

The only person you have much hope of changing in the long run is yourself. So consider how difficult it is to change yourself, and you will have an idea of the difficulty in changing others. As Leo Tolstoy, a

Russian writer, philosopher, and social activist, said, "Everyone thinks of changing the world, but no one thinks of changing himself."

Try this exercise on your own. Think of the best and most long-term mature relationship you currently have. Is there at least one thing about that person that you would like to change and most probably have tried to change? Ask yourself if you have been able to change that one thing. Chances are you have not. As stated in the next key point, people make conscious decisions about their behavior, not just because we want them to do so. So don't waste a lot of time trying to change or control another person. It is better to understand them and work within that parameter than to expend lots of energy trying to get them to change solely because you want them to do so. The major exception to this rule occurs when applying it to situations involving young, developing children. But beware that you don't continue this exception beyond its expiration date. Remember, people most often do things for their reasons, not yours.

People Make Conscious Decisions about Their Behavior

Putting aside for the moment the tendency to sometimes react without thinking, people who think make conscious decisions about their behavior—unless they are mentally ill! So you may be thinking, "Then some of the people I deal with must be mentally ill!" Actually, most people are wired only to do things that they believe are right or just. Others may find certain behaviors hard to rationalize, but it is very difficult for the mentally well person to behave in a way he or she cannot rationalize as correct. *Most people's behavior is reasonable to them.* It may not make sense to others, but it makes sense to that person, in that situation, at that particular point in time. The behavior meets some need of theirs. Different people look at different things from their own perspectives. Behaviors like riots, looting, school shootings, terrorist acts, etc., may seem illogical to most of us, but most of the participants in such events rationalize their behavior as just and right in their own minds. *Behavior mostly results from mind-sets within the person.* One may be influenced by outside factors, but the driving force usually comes from within a person.

So how do people make decisions about their behavior? A key point here is that values influence behavior and that a value is something for which one is willing to make a sacrifice. If you want to know if someone values something, determine what that individual will sacrifice for it.

In my case, I valued getting my bachelor's degree (with a loving and supporting push from my wife, Janis) so much that I was willing to work a full-time day job at General American Life and go to St. Louis University at night to complete my degree. While this choice caused many long days, and I missed many evening events, the bachelor's degree was highly valued. To better understand people, try to understand their values.

I particularly like the work done on values by Dr. Morris Massey.[1] During the 1960s and '70s, Dr. Massey was an associate dean and professor of marketing at the University of Colorado at Boulder. His work at that time focused on values, generations, and what he called significant emotional events (SEEs).

Dr. Massey based a lot of his work on the idea that *What You Are Is Where You Were When*. In other words, the time you were born and raised affects your values. When I began my professional career at General American Life in 1967, there was an elderly lady (Mary Mildred Merritt) nearing retirement working alongside me in the Accounting Department. She had grown up during the Great Depression era and thus was very frugal. The other group of "young whippersnappers" (as she described us) and I, having grown up in a more prosperous period, were not so frugal. This difference in values was clearly illustrated when one of our new and young associates was being disciplined and, as a penalty, was suspended for two days without pay. To Mary Mildred, two days off without pay was an unthinkable disaster. Whereas the younger associate not only did not consider it a disaster but asked if he could have a Friday and Monday as the days of suspension so he could have a long weekend! A different set of values caused a totally different viewpoint of the discipline.

Dr. Massey identified three major periods during which values are developed. These were the imprint period (age zero to seven), the modeling period (age eight to thirteen), and the socialization period (between thirteen and twenty-one). He also discussed how significant emotional events (SEEs) can cause our values to change as we go through life. Significant emotional events might include the following: getting married or divorced, joining the armed forces, having a child, having a grandchild, etc. For me personally, I remember when I *used to* scorn people showing

---

[1]   Morris Massey, *What You Are Is Where You Were When—But Not What You Have to Be*, Audio Cassette (Chicago: Nightingale-Conant, 1972).

pictures of their grandchildren. Now guess who is always showing pictures of his granddaughter? Having a grandchild is definitely a SEE.

Another important work that may help you better understand human behavior comes from the work of the Menninger Clinic.[2] Dr. W. Walter Menninger studied what happens to people when they make a significant role change. Menninger was engaged to study the morale in the Peace Corps. President Kennedy and the leaders of the Peace Corps were concerned about "the level of depression in the Peace Corps." Menninger's study, however, indicated there was no depression in the Peace Corps. Rather, there was a high level of anger. This anger was based on the fact that 97 percent of the volunteers were not doing what they expected, and most were very disillusioned. There were even some reports that one group of Peace Corps volunteers was planning to overthrow the government of their host country, not exactly what the leaders of the Peace Corps had in mind.

The results of this study indicate that people going through significant role changes (or what Massey calls significant emotional events) follow predictable patterns called stations. Many different scholars and consultants have looked at this study and come up with similar conclusions, but sometimes with different names. I favor the following interpretation:

- Arrival—the initial stage of a role change. This is the honeymoon period. It is the beginning, a time of high positive expectations. If not full of positive expectations, why would the change be made?
- Engagement—this is when recognition of reality hits. Things are almost never as expected, and morale plunges often result. The degree of the slide depends largely on how big the gap is between what was expected and what is the actual reality.
- Acceptance—a key time when one makes a decision whether to apply positive energy and accept the responsibility for the role change and all that comes along with it or to abandon the role change. Menninger advises that abandoning the role change can contaminate future changes.
- Reentry—depending on the choices made at the acceptance stage, the individual is either ready or not ready for the next role change.

---

[2]   W. Walter Menninger, *Bulletin of the Menninger Clinic* 52, no. 3 (May 1988): 198-210, accessed January 14, 2014, http://psycnet.apa.org/psycinfo/1989-15533-001.

While this study was primarily based on the Peace Corps, I believe it is relevant to today's business and personal relationships. The key point is to recognize when people in your life are going through these stages and to help them through the difficult but predictable stages of the morale curve.

One other key point: don't predict the curve, as in, "I know you are happy now about this change, but in three months I expect you will be in the dumps." Rather, it is better to help people recognize the curve once they are in it and then help them through it.

If handled well, the role change can launch the individual to a new level of effectiveness. If the role change is handled poorly, as noted above, it may reduce the level of effectiveness and possibly contaminate future role changes.

Using BASIC Skills for Better Behavior Choices

So if we can't have ongoing control over how others act, and people who are responding rather than reacting make conscious decisions about their behavior based on their values and life stages, what can we do? I suggest we need to use our BASIC skills to better understand them and to help them make the best choices. Following are some practical ideas on how to accomplish this.

The Only Way to Get the Best of an Argument Is to Avoid It

In the year 2001, I was asked by a friend and business associate to attend the twelve-week Dale Carnegie flagship course entitled Effective Communications and Human Relations Skills for Success. My friend John Brown owned the Dale Carnegie franchise in Kansas City and asked me to attend the course to give him feedback from a participant's viewpoint. At the time, my friend and business partner Bob Dinkins and I had just sold our company (Human Dynamics) to an Irish firm and were adjusting to being employees versus owners. Although I really couldn't see a lot of potential benefit in taking the Dale Carnegie Course, I agreed to do it as a favor to John. Boy, was I wrong about the value of this course. It was great, life changing, and something I still often recommend to others. I saw much personal growth in myself and in the others in my class. So much so that I volunteered to be a graduate assistant for the next class.

I found much of what I had discovered in my work with the national seminar company had been originally published by Dale Carnegie in the 1930s and 1940s. Perhaps the most profound single lesson I learned during the Dale Carnegie experience was the quote that leads this section.

The only way to get the best of an argument
is to avoid it.

As I pondered this gem of wisdom, I thought back to all the arguments/disagreements I had with my wife, my children, my work associates and asked myself how many times I had won the argument. You can probably guess the answer—close to zero, if not absolutely zero! It dawned on me that we can seldom win an argument because arguments and disagreements are seldom about the truth.

Rather, arguments are about each person's perception of the truth. And as most of us know, our perceptions are our reality. So the lesson here is to avoid arguing with the people in your life. Agree to disagree and move forward on that with which you can agree. Arguing only causes the emotional defenses to be raised and almost always stops positive discussion/communication. So no matter what, try not to argue with the important people in your life.

Although surely not totally relevant to all situations, consider the old saying, "Never wrestle with a pig because you both get dirty and only the pig likes it." Or if you prefer a more direct approach, from Steve Gilliland's book *Hits of Humor*, "Do not argue with an idiot. He will drag you down to his level and beat you with experience."

What Gets Rewarded Is What Gets Done

So if we can't have ongoing control over how others act and people make conscious decisions about their behavior and the only way to get the best of an argument is to avoid it, what must we do or understand to keep and improve the relationships with the key people in our lives?

The first step is to better understand what motivates others. Given an appropriate level of personal caring, civilized behavior, and reasonably fair compensation in the workplace (or attention in personal settings), motivation is something that comes from within an individual. Abraham Maslow's theory is that we are wanting animals and that our behavior is determined by unsatisfied needs that we want to satisfy. Thus, satisfied needs do not normally motivate us.

We don't really motivate people to do things; rather, we create conditions that cause them to want to do what we want them to do. The environment will either encourage the desired behavior or discourage it. I have always liked the flower analogy when thinking about motivation. What is the best way to make a flower grow? There is clearly one way not to make a flower grow—reaching down and pulling it up. Rather, it is much better to influence the flower's environment by putting fertilizer on it (not too much!), tilling the soil, adding water, keeping it away from other environmental negatives, getting it into the sunlight, etc.

People, like flowers, also benefit more from nourishing, positive environments and periodic positive attention than they do from being pulled. It is best to create an environment in which the other person can grow. Motivation is not something one does to other people; rather, it is providing an environment in which people grow themselves.

We must remove barriers and create a climate that allows people to grow. An important element of this process is to treat people the way you want them to become. You can't treat your kids like kids all the time and expect them one day to magically wake up as adults. You need to be shaping them for adulthood during the process.

The title concept of this section comes from a book entitled *The Greatest Management Principle in the World* by Dr. Michael LeBoeuf.[3] See his website for more detailed information at http://www.michaelleboeuf.com/.

Dr. LeBoeuf believed the greatest management principle in the world is "the things that get rewarded get done"—or stated another way, *the behavior you reward is the behavior you get.* Dr. LeBoeuf's book, although written many years ago, includes many specific examples of how this reward concept works in the real world. Dr. LeBoeuf illustrates this concept with the fisherman, frog, and snake parable that follows.

---

[3] Dr. Michael LeBoeuf, *The Greatest Management Principle in the World* (New York: G. P. Putnam's Group, 1985), 23.

A man went fishing one day. He looked over the side of his boat and saw a snake with a frog in its mouth. Feeling sorry for the frog, he reached down, gently took the frog from the snake, and set the frog free. But then he felt sorry for the snake. He looked around the boat, but he had no food. All he had was a bottle of bourbon. So he opened the bottle and gave the snake a few shots. The snake went off happy, the frog was happy, and the man was happy to have performed such good deeds. He thought everything was great until about ten minutes passed and he heard something knock against the side of his boat. With stunned disbelief, the fisherman looked down and saw the snake was back with two frogs!

As Dr. LeBoeuf explains, the parable contains two important lessons: First, you get more of the behavior that you reward. You don't get what you hope for, ask for, wish for, or beg for. You get what you reward. Come what may, all living beings are going to act in their own best self-interest, and it's unrealistic to expect them to do otherwise.

And second, in trying to do the right thing, it's oh so easy to fall into the trap of inadvertently rewarding the wrong behavior and getting the wrong results.

By and large, people behave the way the reward system teaches them to behave. And it's true for the executive, the salesperson, the janitor, your partner, your child, or anyone else.

Dr. LeBoeuf notes, you would think that such a simple, obvious principle would be well adhered to in most organizations. Guess again! The single greatest obstacle to effective performance in most organizations is the giant mismatch between the behavior needed and the behavior rewarded. Organizations of all kinds fall into the trap of hoping for A, rewarding B, and wondering why they get B.

Although coming from a management or leadership book, this concept applies to all the roles we play. The key lesson is learning what and how to reward. Dr. LeBoeuf writes that we need to find the answer to three crucial questions:

- What behavior do I want?
- How will I recognize it?
- How will I reward it?

The behaviors that we want vary by the situation and the role we are playing. As to recognition and reward in the business world, we tend to default to money as the ultimate recognition or reward. Yet many studies have challenged money as the key motivator, stating that money has short-term, limited motivational power. Assuming one's essential compensation and job security needs are met, then motivation in the workplace comes mostly from feeling we are recognized and appreciated and are part of something important and stimulating.

Recognition in the partner and parenting roles also usually comes mostly from recognition and appreciation. The most visual sign of our recognition and appreciation of partners and children is the quantity and quality of time we allow for them. Our time is the most precious gift we can give the other important people in our lives.

Model the Behavior You Desire

Simply stated, you cannot be late to meetings, use cigarettes, illegal drugs, or consume alcohol in excess if you don't want others in your life to do the same.

Try not to overreact to noncritical situations. Remember the Rollo May quote:

> Real human freedom is the ability to pause
> between the events of our lives and
> choose how we will respond.

Realize that a good example has twice the advantage of good advice. Remember the old saying, "Sometimes I can't hear you because your actions drown out your words." As best as you can, model the behavior you desire from the others in your life. They are watching you all the time, and do as I say, not as I do doesn't normally lead to positive results. I know Jennifer watched and learned from the high level of caring Janis provided Missy. Jennifer had a great model for her own eventual motherhood role.

The 80/10/10 Rule

No behavioral theory is perfect or works in every situation. Thus the need to be situational in all relationships (more on being situational later under the *S*). While not getting hung up on the exact percentages, understand that the concepts being discussed in this section (and throughout the book) apply about 80 percent of the time to 80 percent of the people. Recognize that there are about 10 percent of the people who 80 percent of the time will respond positively to just about any situation they encounter regardless of other factors, including what you do or do not do. Another 10 percent of people are just the opposite. Meaning that this group will be challenged to respond positively to almost any situation they encounter, most of the time. My experience leads me to believe that the ideas being discussed in this book will resonate positively with 80 percent of the people, 80 percent of the time.

Understand Behavior—Summary

Don't waste your time and resources trying to change someone else. When others are being difficult, they are doing it for some sort of payoff. A payoff that only they may understand. You must accept that you cannot change another person for the long run. They will and must make their own decisions to change. These decisions will ultimately be based more on their own value systems—values that you can help shape and develop. Realize that while you can't change other people's behavior, you can learn how to change your behavior so that you can work with or around them and prevent them from manipulating you. Rather than trying to change someone else's behavior, spend your time understanding where they are coming from and what you can do to reward the desired behavior. Realize the value of avoiding arguments. Remember, what gets rewarded is what gets done. Understand the buyer's benefit rule: if there is no benefit to the other person, the other person is less likely to want to behave in the desired way. It also helps if the other person clearly understands what is expected and agrees to any significant changes.

Here is a personal story about the need to be responsible for your own behavior. My first year in high school was traumatic. Baden School was a small, local neighborhood elementary school. I could walk to and from school. I knew almost everyone. I earned and received good grades.

The transition to Beaumont High School was difficult at best. To get to Beaumont, I had to walk uphill both ways in the snow, with no shoes! Well, not really, however, I did have to take the public bus system, which involved a transfer from one bus route to another and took almost an hour each way. Beaumont High was very large. There was a lot of racial tension (and a couple of riots). While I had been a good student at Baden, my first semester at Beaumont resulted in less than spectacular final grades. I received and "earned" three Cs, one D, and one F. The D was in beginning algebra, and I now realize it also should have been an F. Passing me on to the next level of math when I was not ready contributed to a lifelong struggle with higher level math. I remember how disappointed my mom and dad were with me about these grades. I also remember this as a wake-up call for me—a realization that only I could be ultimately responsible for my success or lack of same. The truly earned and clearly awakening moment for me was the F in introduction to Spanish. My teacher, Mr. Ralph Wilcox, called me aside at the time and told me he knew I could do much better and that he expected me to repeat the Spanish class. Once I took responsibility for my own success, high school and Spanish specifically became much more enjoyable. By the end of my second semester of introduction to Spanish, I was tutoring other students.

Keep Balance in Your Personal and Professional Life

The second *B* in the BASIC strategy represents the very important concept of balance. All the BASIC concepts can be undermined if we are unable to keep a proper balance in both our personal and professional lives. Think of ice skating and how important balance is in this process—not just to stay upright (which I'm not very good at!) but also the balance required to move forward. Meaning one leg going in direction A, the other in direction B, resulting in moving forward in the desired direction C.

Following are the key concepts of keeping balance in your personal life:

- Understand what causes stress.
- Live in the present.
- Keep your perspective.
- Seek and use humor for energy.

Understand What Causes Stress

We must learn how to manage and deal with stress. Stress can cause us to be out of balance and make it much more difficult to practice all the other elements of the BASIC formula. Managing stress is a key component of taking care of ourselves and our health, which should be one, if not the highest, of our priorities. Good health is everyone's major source of wealth. Without good health, happiness and success are more difficult. The key here is to understand what causes stress. If

Stress!!!

you ask a group of people what causes stress, the answers will usually include such things as traffic, deadlines, travel delays, budgets, taxes, bosses, coworkers, spouses, etc. Events and circumstances such as these that most people say cause stress really have little to do with our stress.

Events and circumstances occur all the time. It is our chosen reaction, our point of view, that really causes stress. Every study I have seen says the number 1 cause of stress is our own point of view about happenings in our life. It is our chosen point of view, our expectations, our attitudes that most often affect how we react to or feel about the events and circumstances we encounter. Whatever circumstance we find ourselves in, we have a choice as to how we want to look at that circumstance. Most everything that happens to us in life represents our choices. As Rollo May said,

> Real human freedom is the ability to pause
> between the events of our lives and
> choose how we will respond.

He goes on to point out that we are the only animal in the kingdom that has this ability to make a conscious choice as to how we will respond. And yet often we just react instead of choosing.

The simple formula is that events + reaction = outcomes. We can control the outcome by our reaction to the events. Try to be proactive, not reactive. Proactive behavior means thinking before acting (choice). Reactive behavior means acting before thinking.

Live in the Present

Living in the present is a particularly challenging task for many, including me. I often find myself worrying about something that happened in the past or looking ahead to something that may happen in the future and thus not fully embracing the present. Dale Carnegie called being in the present moment living in day-tight compartments. Abraham Maslow described living in the present as a major element of mental wellness. Often, however, many of us have one foot in the past, worrying about things we can't change, and the other foot out in the future, worrying about things that might happen or won't happen as we anticipate, or are just uncontrollable by us. This puts us in a very vulnerable and fragile state.

In his book *Productivity Power*, my friend and colleague Jim Temme, references an article in the *Office Professional* magazine. This article reported that only about 2 percent of the average person's worrying time is spent on anything that might be helped or somehow improved by worrying. The other 98 percent of the time is spent (wasted) as follows:

- Forty percent on things that never happen.
- Thirty-five percent on things that can't be changed.
- Fifteen percent on things that turn out better than expected.
- Eight percent on useless, petty worries.

Jim adds that it's useless to worry about the trivial matters and about things that are unlikely to happen. It is better to put worry thoughts out of our mind and to replace them with productive thoughts.

Given our inclination to live in the past and simultaneously worry about the future, we are often straddling the present, which is a very uncomfortable position. Try not to dwell on the should haves of the past and try to limit your anxiety and fear about the future. Remember that fear is often just **f**alse **e**xpectations **a**ppearing **r**eal.

Here are a few other relevant quotes on living in the present.

From an accounting viewpoint by Kay Lyons:

> Yesterday is a cancelled check.
> Tomorrow is a promissory note.
> Today is the only cash you have,
> so spend it wisely.

From a historical viewpoint by Alice Morse Earle:

> The clock is running.
> Make the most of today.
> Time waits for no man.
> Yesterday is history.
> Tomorrow is a mystery.
> Today is a gift.
> That's why it is called the present.

As to living in the future, Mark Twain said it well:

> I have been through some terrible things in my life,
> some of which actually happened.

Many writers have emphasized the importance of living in and enjoying the present. We often spend too much time waiting for tomorrow.

As John Lennon said, "Life is what happens along the way while you're making other plans." Life truly is what happens when we are making other plans or having other thoughts about the past or future.

Keep Your Perspective

The following is a letter received from a college student:

Dear Mom:

I thought I'd write to let you know what has been going on here at school.

Don't get worried but my arm is in a cast. I broke it yesterday when I had to jump out of the dorm window because of the fire that was accidentally started when Mary and I got too high smoking pot. They kept us in jail overnight.

It doesn't matter that it's my writing hand that is broken because I'm going to quit school next week and marry Johnny anyway. Johnny's father has offered him a partnership in his gas station in Alaska and it sounds swell.

There is an extra room over the station, which will be large enough, at least until the baby comes in a few months. Alaska has a strong Alcoholics Anonymous program, which should help Johnny a lot.

> Our only concern is that the Symbionese Liberation Army doesn't have an active chapter there—yet.
>
> P.S.
>
> My arm is not broken.
>
> There was no fire.
>
> I don't smoke dope.
>
> I wasn't in jail.
>
> I'm not quitting school or getting married.
>
> I'm not going to Alaska.
>
> I'm not pregnant.
>
> And, I'm not a political extremist.
>
> However, I did get a "D" in chemistry and I just wanted you to be able to put things in their proper perspective!

The fictional letter above has been around for a long time. However, in a humorous way, it does point out the importance of keeping our perspective.

Here is an adaptation of a famous perceptual illusion from an anonymous 1888 German postcard in which the brain switches between seeing a young girl and an old woman (or wife and mother-in-law).

Mark Twain once suggested the following regarding keeping one's perspective and avoiding procrastination:

> If you know you have to swallow a frog,
> swallow it first thing in the morning.
> If there are two frogs, swallow the big one first.

When things start getting hectic, back off, try to look at things from a proper perspective. Ask yourself, will this really matter down the road? Happiness is really a matter of habit. Here is another tidbit from Dale Carnegie on how to face trouble:[4]

- Ask yourself, "What is the worst thing that can possibly happen?"
- Prepare to accept the worst.
- Try to improve the worst.
- Remind yourself of the exorbitant price you can pay for worry in terms of your health.

Many speakers have used the following exercise to demonstrate the power of perspective.

Who Am I?

At the age of:

- 22 I failed in business.
- 23 I was defeated for legislature.
- 24 I failed in business again.
- 26 My fiancé died.
- 27 I had a nervous breakdown.
- 29 I was defeated again for public office.
- 31 I was defeated in run for Congress.
- 34 I was defeated in run for Congress.
- 39 I was defeated in run for Congress.
- 46 I was defeated in run for U.S. Senate.
- 47 I was defeated in run for Vice President of the U.S.
- 49 I was defeated in run for U.S. Senate.
- 51 I was elected President of the U.S.

---

[4] Dale Carnegie, "Overcoming Worry," *Dale Carnegie Training,* accessed January 14, 2014, http://www.dcarnegietraining.com/resources/overcoming-worry

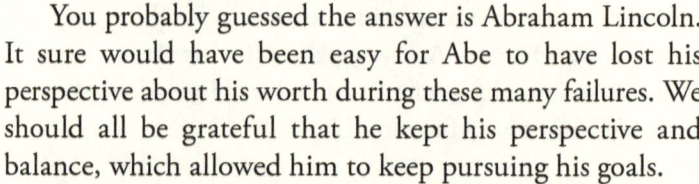

You probably guessed the answer is Abraham Lincoln. It sure would have been easy for Abe to have lost his perspective about his worth during these many failures. We should all be grateful that he kept his perspective and balance, which allowed him to keep pursuing his goals.

Another aspect of perspective is our natural inclination to assume whether current events are good or bad. Usually we have a tendency to assume the worst. Here is an old Chinese fable that illustrates this point.

> - This fable really has no beginning or no end.
> - A farmer and his son had only one horse.
> - This horse that they loved jumped the fence one day and ran way. Is this good or bad?
> - Two months later the beloved horse returned leading 100 other wild stallions behind it. Is this good or bad?
> - The very next day, the son breaks his leg trying to train one of the wild stallions. Is this good or bad?
> - The following month the country goes to war but the son cannot go to war because of his broken leg. Is this good or bad?
> - Later they learn that the entire troop the son would have joined is wiped out in a battle. Is this good or bad?

As Shakespeare said,

Nothing is good or bad—but thinking makes it so.

The moral of this fable is that some of the best things that happen to people have happened because of something they did not originally want to happen or that they perceive as bad. Here is a personal example. In 1992 I was a member of the board of directors and executive staff at the Frankona America Reinsurance companies. Since joining Frankona in 1979, I advanced quickly up the ladder of success. But then it became apparent in 1992 that my career path was blocked, and I was blocking the path of others reporting to me. To their great credit, my then bosses,

Dr. Achim Kann and Dr. Karl Mayr, recognized the situation and approached me about finding other employment. At the time it seemed to be really bad news, but as it turned out, they helped me start my own company, which was quite successful, and the change also led to many other additional opportunities and career enhancements and ultimately to my writing this book.

It is also important that we try to help others in our life keep their perspective—although this is not always within our control. I remember when Jennifer was about seven years old, Janis and I decided to purchase a big girl bedroom set for her. After much shopping around and squeezing some pennies, we were on our way to purchase the selected bedroom set. I wanted to impress on Jennifer what a big purchase this was and how she would need to take good care of this significant investment. I carefully explained to her, "Daddy will have to work two weeks to pay for the new furniture." Her quick reply from the backseat was priceless, "You mean I'll have to wait two weeks to get the new furniture!" Not the message I had in mind, but also a good reminder of how perspective is driven by each person's viewpoint. By the way, we still have that same bedroom set.

Seek and Use Humor for Energy

Humor is a great tool to help us keep things in balance. Funny friends, books, magazines, movies, comic strips, YouTube videos, as well as laughs on the job and in the family setting are important energizers for all of us. Humor, however, must be appropriate to the situation and not at the expense of others. I did hear a speaker once come close to crossing this line. He told the story of a recent homicide detectives convention wherein he reported that the number 1 selling trinket at the convention was a button that read, "Our day begins when yours ends." I am not sure if this wasn't just a made-up story to get a laugh, though it does illustrate the fine line we must walk when using humor. Obviously one would want to be very aware of where and how this story was told.

Sometime ago, I saw an official-looking police-like T-shirt. The front side had an official police-type logo. On the back it said, "Bomb Squad— if you see me running, try to keep up!"

As illustrated above, it is very important to keep balance in your personal life. It is equally important to keep balance in your professional life. Following are the key concepts of keeping balance in your professional life:

- Balance interpersonal and technical skills.
- Beware of the tyranny of the urgent.
- Don't confuse activity with results.
- Don't be a wandering generality.

Balance Interpersonal and Technical Skills

Many years ago, the Carnegie Institute conducted a study of the skills that are needed to advance in one's chosen profession. From my view, the key finding of this study is that once you are in your chosen profession and have proven you have the necessary basic technical skills, your future advancement is likely to be 85 percent based on your interpersonal and administrative skills and only 15 percent based on your technical skills. Technical skills are those with a professional focus (math, science, engineering, programming, etc.). Interpersonal skills are those needed to work effectively with others. Administrative skills are those needed to deal with the inevitable bureaucracy of organizations (forms, politics, power, etc.)

Although one could certainly debate the exact percentages, I have often seen technical people limited by their lack of interpersonal and administrative skills. Think back over your career. How many times have you seen someone with excellent technical skills that stalled on the way up the ladder due to lacking the needed interpersonal and administrative skills?

There are three elements of interpersonal skills. These are your intentions, the perceptions of others, and your behavior. No one knows your intentions except you. Perceptions are what the others see. They are in the eye of the beholder. Your behavior is what you do to make your intentions happen. Other people will believe the behavior they see. For maximum results, you must be clear on what you want to achieve and pick the behavior needed to achieve this.

There is an old story that illustrates the problems with being too technical or overusing technical skills. It seems back in the time of the French Revolution, there were three individuals sentenced to die via the guillotine. The first was a government official. He was given a last chance to speak and said, "Long live the king." His head was then placed into the guillotine, and the executioner released the blade. However, the blade stopped three inches short of his neck. The crowd, thinking it must be a sign from above, chanted, "Let him go." And so the executioner freed him. The second person scheduled to be executed this same day was a church official who, when given his last chance to speak, said, "Long live the pope." His head was then placed into the guillotine, and the executioner released the blade. The blade stopped three inches short of his neck as well. Again, the crowd, thinking it must be a miracle from above, shouted, "Let him go." And so the executioner did. The third person to be executed this day was a technical person. When given his last chance to speak, he said, "You know, if you loosened that top screw . . ." Truly sometimes being overly technical can be a bad thing.

One other related point is that most agree the need for technical skills most often goes down as an individual goes up the organizational ladder. Most also agree that the need for administrative skills increases as one goes up the organizational ladder. And many contend that the need for interpersonal skills is lesser at the higher levels, if one gets to the higher levels. In other words, often one can get away with less people skills as they go up, if they go up. Daddy Warbucks in the Broadway play *Annie* said, "You don't have to be nice to people on the way up—if you don't plan to see them again on the way down." I am not sure I agree with this theory that one does not need as much interpersonal skills as one advances up the organization. I'm more in the camp of Zig Ziglar (author, salesman, and motivational speaker) who said, "Ability can take you to the top, but it takes character to keep you there."

Beware of the Tyranny of the Urgent

As Stephen Covey and many others have said, we need to put first things first. Many times, our planned important items are replaced by the urgent events of our days. Urgency is a function of time. Importance is a function of value. Charles Hummel has written extensively on the tyranny of the urgent, including the following:

> Urgent things are seldom important and
> important things are seldom urgent.

Failing to recognize and control the tyranny of the urgent can seriously affect our effectiveness. Try to focus on the significant few and avoid the trivial many. Focus on the important items as much as possible.

Don't Confuse Activity with Results

We must constantly be aware of the difference between being busy and being effective. It is more valuable to be doing the right thing than doing the thing right. An old adage says, "It is not so much how busy you are, but why you are busy. The bee is praised and the mosquito swatted."

Don't confuse activity with results. Activities are what we do, and results are what we accomplish. Be wary of spending your days doing chores rather than doing things that will move you more toward your goals.

Work smarter, not just harder. Effectiveness is not directly related to effort. Effectiveness does not result from doing more; rather, it is a product of doing less but doing it better.

Don't Be a Wandering Generality—Establish Goals

Yogi Berra, the great Yankees catcher, once said,

> You've got to be very careful
> if you don't know where you are going,
> because you might get there.

Goals are essential to being productive and to adding balance into our personal and professional lives. Goals are the measuring rod of importance. Goals should be results, not activities. If you don't have and monitor goals, how can you know what is truly important? Time is like a closet. If you don't decide on what goes in there, it will fill up with junk.

As Lily Tomlin once said,

> I always wanted to be somebody—
> now I realize I should have been more specific.

Knowing where you are going is half the journey. Many times we just do not know enough about where we are going. Goals provide a track to run on. They provide a line of sight that enables us to see the connection between our efforts and our rewards. Here are three very important questions to ask when establishing goals:

- Where am I?
- Where do I want to go?
- How do I get there?

Always strive to create SMART goals. The SMART criteria have been around in many forms for many years. Some attribute the original version to Peter Drucker.

- Specific—concisely worded and communicates precisely what is expected.
- Measurable—includes specific measurements, observable results. If you can't determine if the goal was met, it is too vague.
- Attainable—a stretch but doable and motivating.
- Relevant—tied to organizational or people-related goals and within the scope of your control.
- Time Limited—tied to completion within a certain time frame ("a goal is a dream with a deadline"—Diana Scharf Hunt).

GOALS

S	Specific
M	Measurable
A	Attainable
R	Relevant
T	Time Limited

Zig Ziglar demonstrated the value of goals by referencing a study of Harvard graduates wherein the 3 percent that had written specific goals outperformed (financially) the other 97 percent of their class twenty years later. Scott Reid writes the following on the importance of goal setting:

> This one step—choosing a goal and sticking to it—
> changes everything.

Keep Balance in Your Personal & Professional Life—Summary

Coming back to the ice skating analogy that opened this chapter (from Aak Brakel in his work entitled *People and Organizations Interacting*), recall the balance required to move forward. Meaning one leg going in direction A, the other in direction B, and you move forward in direction C. Think of how much balance and coordinated effort is involved to stay upright and move in the desired direction. Think of direction A as work and B as nonwork or personal time and C as your overall destination in life. Or think of A as your technical skills and B as your interpersonal skills and C as your career advancement objectives. If A and/or B are neglected or aren't properly balanced and coordinated, your course is changed or distorted. Be sure to appropriately value the need for interpersonal and administrative skills, be wary of the tyranny of the urgent, don't confuse activity with results, and create and monitor goals. It is important to set personal and professional goals to achieve a balance between your work and personal life.

Ask yourself, when was the last time you really relaxed or loafed? If this question is too easy, or too hard, to answer, you might want to take another look at the balance in your life. A good definition of relaxation is the ability to do absolutely nothing and feel good about it. I retired from full-time work on January 1, 2014. I have to admit that truly relaxing, as defined herein, is going to require a little period of adjustment. Recognizing and acknowledging this shortfall on my part represents the first step in addressing this vulnerability of mine.

One last thought on keeping your balance concerns what to do when we are in a situation that we don't like. There are really only three healthy options for situations we don't like:

1. Change—either try to improve the situation or redefine it. If you try but can't change the situation, move to step 2.
2. Accept—decide to truly accept the situation. Do not moan about it. If you can't accept it, move to step 3.
3. Leave—if you can't leave the situation, then the only healthy solution is to go back and reevaluate steps 1 and 2.

In order to reach a healthy solution, you must choose one of the three options.

Don't be like the monk who was a member of an order that only allowed him to speak to the head monk (abbot) once every twenty years. After completing his first twenty years, he got his turn to speak and simply said, "Room too hot." The abbot acknowledged his comment and sent him back to work. Another twenty years passed, and on his second occasion to talk with the abbot, the monk said, "Food bad." Again the abbot acknowledged his comment and then dismissed him back to his tasks. On the sixtieth year of his time at the monastery, the monk had one more chance to talk with the abbot. This time he said, "I quit." The abbot looked at him and said, "Good, all you've done since you've been here is complain!"

Begin Each Circumstance Anew

The *A* in the BASIC strategy represents *anew*. Begin each situation anew. Meaning with a proper balance between our past experiences and the new circumstances.

Following are the key concepts of beginning each circumstance anew:

- Call on past experiences, but assess each circumstance anew.
- Avoid stereotyping.
- Watch for preconceived negative biases.
- Make the essential transition to leadership.
- Think of parents as leaders.

Call on Past Experiences, but Assess Each Circumstance Anew

> In times of rapid change, experience could be your worst enemy.
> —J. Paul Getty

J. Paul Getty founded the Getty Oil Company, and in 1957, *Fortune Magazine* named him one of the richest living Americans. While he very much valued experience among his colleagues and workers, he was also quite aware that experience can also mislead in some circumstances. Oscar Wilde, on assumptions, said, "When you assume, you make an ass out of u and me." (Ass, u, me.)

The point here is to value your past experience but to also test each new circumstance for current applicability of that past experience.

Anthony Robbins, a world-renowned author, speaker, and peak performance strategist, often talks about how success ultimately comes from experience when he says the following:

- Success is the result of good judgment.

- Good judgment is the result of experience.
- Experience is the result of bad judgment.

There are innumerable examples of "experts" who have been stuck in their current experiences and failed to see the situation anew. Here are a few examples:

- "Everything of significance has been invented."—Director of U.S. Patent Office (1890)
- "Who the hell wants to hear actors speak?"—Henry Warner, Warner Brothers Studios (1927)
- "Sensible and responsible women don't want to vote."—Grover Cleveland Alexander (1905)
- "I think there is a world market for maybe five computers."—Thomas Watson, chairman of IBM (1943)
- "There is no reason anyone would want a computer in their home."—Ken Olson, president of Digital Equipment Corporation (1977)
- "The media's great love affair with the Nintendo Wii is beginning to sour. There are whispers that the device is tiring and gimmicky."—Tyler Todd, video game columnist *Montreal Gazette* (2006)
- "Amazon is a stock that continues to live on borrowed time."—Tim Boyd, Caris and Co. (2006)

The world is full of verbal, visual, and other distortions that can cause confusion and mislead us. For instance, here is an exercise I often use to begin a workshop. Using only your eyes, count the number of times the letter *F* appears in the following sentence.

FINISHED FILES ARE THE RE-
SULT OF YEARS OF SCIENTIF-
IC STUDY COMBINED WITH THE
EXPERIENCE OF MANY YEARS.

How many letter Fs did you count? If you counted less than six, count again. How many do you see now? Keep trying until you find all six Fs. (If you cannot find all six Fs, the correct answer is illustrated in the summary section of this chapter.)

Our misconceptions, based on our past experiences, most likely will never rise to the level of incorrectness of the quotes cited above. Maybe the F count is just a fun example of what can be. But we must carefully monitor for negative and/or preconceived ideas. While we don't want to ignore our past experiences, we must always test them for correct and current applicability. Try to enter each new opportunity without bias from the past and minimize or avoid preconceived ideas. It is also very important to monitor our attitudes. Attitudes are simply the feelings we choose to remember. Make sure your attitude is appropriate for the given situation. François-Marie Arouet (Voltaire), a French Enlightenment writer, historian, and philosopher, said,

> The most important decision we make each day
> is to be in a good mood.

Here is a riddle for your consideration. What am I thinking of?
- George Bush has a short one.
- Mikhail Gorbachev has a long one.
- Neither Cher nor Madonna has one.
- The pope has one but, for religious reasons, cannot use his.

The right answer, of course, is a last name. What were you thinking? Be careful of those preconceived ideas.

Avoid Stereotyping

When we are stereotyping, we are assigning meaning based on our past experiences/knowledge. Again, this failure to begin anew can be limiting in our relationships with others. I remember attending an industry meeting many years back and seeing several attendees wearing white socks with dark business suits. Based on my past experience/ knowledge, this meant to me that they were not very smart dressers and, therefore, by extension, not very smart businesspeople. My experience/ knowledge was based on Janis having schooled me on the properness of dark socks with a dark business suit. I had only worn a suit one time (for my elementary school graduation) prior to getting married. So based on my assumptions, I assumed that these attendees were insignificant. Well, it turned out they were from another culture that did not have the same dress code as I did, and they were there starting the process of buying up some of the companies of those wearing the dark socks. Obviously my stereotyping was off base.

Effective people have an open mind and avoid labeling. According to many sources on the Internet, Frank Zappa, an American musician, bandleader, songwriter, composer, and film director, once said, "A man's mind is like a parachute; to work, it must be open."

Watch for Preconceived Negative Biases

In the last year of my full-time professional work, Dave Wine, president of MAX Insurance (www.maxinsurance.com), sponsored a momentivity workshop for all our employees. This workshop was delivered by Maria Hunt of Avila University. Initially this opportunity reminded me a lot of my initial response to the Dale Carnegie program discussed earlier in this book. My first thoughts were preconceived negatives about what more could I learn from this experience. Again, I was wrong and I learned a lot. I was particularly intrigued by how our brain works and why and how the brain sets us up for preconceived negative bias.

For more in-depth discussion of this topic, see the "Mindfulness and Momentivity" work of Maria Hunt of Avila University at http:// transformlearning.avila.edu/mindfulness/.

The part of Maria's excellent work that supports most nicely the BASIC strategy revolves around how the brain works and what we can do to take charge of our brain to avoid our built-in preconceived negative biases.

See the following diagram from Maria's work:

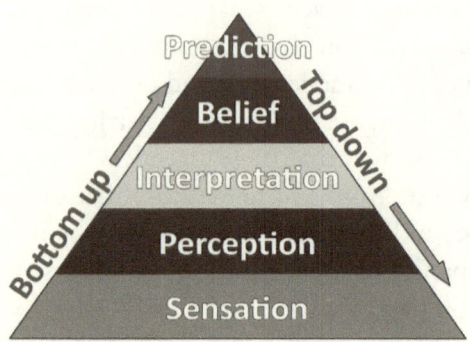

In the diagram, top-down refers to one way that our brain operates. Top-down processing means that we react to a situation using our past assumptions/learnings (prediction) without giving it any mindful attention. Bottom-up processing means we begin with our basic sensations in the moment (sensation, perception—noticing the sights, sounds, smells, etc., that are actually happening); then we move toward making an evaluation of the situation (interpretation). This evaluation or analysis is what then guides the response we choose. This is sometimes called beginner's mind, where we meet each moment on its own merit rather than bringing our previous assumptions into the situation.

Each of these ways our brain operates is very important. We need top-down processing, for example, when we see the brake lights go on in the car driving in front of us. In this situation, it is really good to begin with what we've learned in the past: I see the brake lights, the other car is slowing down, and I'd better put on my brakes!

The problem is that most of us tend to default to this top-down processing, with our brain on autopilot, in most situations. This is only because our brains find it more efficient to operate in this way. What this means though is that we often miss the opportunity for new learning or for making a more effective, novel response. We need an aware and observing mind to take that extra breath, that pregnant pause, and do bottom-up processing. With bottom-up processing, we re-perceive: What are the sensations I am experiencing? What is the perception I have of this?

Then we are able to re-decide what interpretation we might give to a situation. This will, in turn, determine how we choose to respond.

We must understand, however, that if we don't do the bottom-up processing, our brain is a problem solver that most of the time works on autopilot (stimulation-driven), looking for speed and fast process. When working on autopilot, our brain sees what it expects to see, reacts to what should be, and does not seek what is important. Our brain assigns an emotional tag to everything we experience, with a greater weight to negative emotional tags.

This is part of the biological design to keep us safe and alive. Our brain is good at jumping to conclusions, often the negative conclusions (good at awfullizing situations, i.e., defaulting to how awful it can be). We can free ourselves from these habits of our brains only if we are here in the moment (momentivity), paying attention.

For me, Maria's work directly supports the need to pause and decide how we will respond rather than letting the autopilot take over. We can choose our response rather than just letting the brain react. Maria points out that attention is our brain's gatekeeper. We need to train our attitude to pause, consider the situation, and then most often choose to move away from negativity. Negativity is harmful to our health. It reduces what we see. Our world narrows when we are in a negative state. When we are in a positive state, all kinds of opportunities open up to us.

We must keep in mind the difference between a response and a reaction. My colleague Jim Temme says a response is with forethought whereas a reaction is without forethought.

Make the Essential Transition to Leadership

In the preface I explained how this whole BASIC process got started when I was asked to help revise a day-long seminar intended to help technical people better make the transition to leadership. One of the major lessons that comes out of this course for technical people in or moving to a leadership role is: *the characteristics and skills that helped them succeed in a technical role can seriously hinder their chances for maximum success as a leader.* In order to best succeed as a leader, the technical person will have to give up some things that are important to him or her as a technical person to fully enter leadership.

As part of the course, we asked the following question: what do you love about your job as a technical person? Typical answers include the following:

> - Direct involvement in problem solving
> - Clear role definition
> - Measurement of worth based solely on professional competence
> - Control over personal development
> - Being insulated from organizational politics
> - Being on the "cutting edge"
> - Task completion—closure

The follow-up is question number 2: what are/were the payoffs for going into leadership? Typical answers to question number 2 are the following:

> - Additional money
> - Chance for financial security
> - An element of autonomy
> - Chance to be in charge
> - Ability to amplify my efforts
> - Personal growth opportunities
> - Inside knowledge
> - Increased visibility
> - More control

So then the final question is: Did/do you gain enough (payoffs) to offset the give-ups (what they loved)? Those who think they have gained enough are much more likely to be successful making the transition to leadership.

In going into leadership or in fully embracing leadership, we may be leaving something we love and going into something that is, at best, different, and perhaps something less than we expect. Anytime we make a major change in our lives, we leave feelings of security and often feel negative concerns. For more on this subject, see the previous information on Menninger's morale curve studies.

As an example of the effects of change, do the following exercise:

- Sign your name with your natural hand.
- How does that feel? Describe your feelings while signing your name with your natural hand.
- Now sign your name with your opposite hand.
- How does that feel? Describe your feelings while signing your name with the opposite hand.

Most people will describe signing with their natural hand as natural, comfortable, easy, etc. But most describe signing with the other hand as childish, awkward, uncomfortable, etc. If such a minor change as using your opposite hand to sign your name can invoke these feelings, why would we be surprised that other more major life and role changes would have such a strong effect on us?

In the leadership skills for technical people course, we identified several value/motivation shifts that are required for technical people to become effective leaders. In order to make a successful transition from a purely technical person to an effective leader, a technical person must begin anew by moving from a technical emphasis to a more general leadership emphasis.

- From a narrow area of discipline/logic to a wide variety of new ideas.
- From a high degree of specialization to more generalist skills.
- From a low need for social interaction to a high need for same.
- From loyalty to a profession trade or skill to loyalty to an organization.
- From responsibility for their own work to responsibility for the work of others.

Moving from a technical role to a leadership role is crossing a threshold. The technical skills that got the individual to his or her place as a technician can actually hinder them as leaders.

To be most successful, you must make the same level of commitment to improving your leadership skills as you have your technical skills. In my experience, for most technical people, it is very hard to give up the technical publications and meetings in favor of leadership publications and meetings.

Many of the technical skills can be turned into strengths if properly channeled. But leadership does involve reversing powerful technical inclinations, such as

- from details to big picture;
- from production to coalitions and partnerships;
- to seeing the positive role of a solid human relations and support system versus the time and energy demands required by such a system.

Technical people must give up some important technical things in order to maximize their leadership capabilities.

Many of us have a tendency to be perfectionists. I have found this to be especially true for technical people. Perfectionism is not knowing when to stop. When is a perfectionist done? Only when time runs out! You are now reading a real-life personal example of perfectionism at work. If it were not for a publishing timeline, I might still be working to perfect this book. Perfectionism saps energy, steals time, and ultimately negatively impacts success. A perfectionist is someone who takes great pains in everything he or she does and gives those pains to everyone else. As a perfectionist, you need to understand that the people you work and live with are going to be a constant source of disappointment to you. Being the most effective leader, partner, or parent requires us to address this vulnerability.

One can best address this and other vulnerabilities by following a three step process:

1. Recognize the vulnerability.
2. Develop a step-by-step plan for improvement.
3. Express your commitment to address the vulnerability to another person for support and feedback.

Another interesting outcome of the leadership skills for technical people course is a list of the characteristics of the best and worst leaders from the attendee's point of view. These characteristics will be discussed in the "Handle People with Care" chapter of this book.

Think of Parents as Leaders

When I think about the other roles we play as a partner or parent, I believe much of this crossing a threshold theory also applies to the parenting role. In many ways, parents are like the technical person in that they kind of know how most of the intricacies of life tend to work. They are certainly more aware of these items than their children/grandchildren. In the earlier years, we as parents are heavily involved in family problem solving. We have clear role definitions for ourselves and the children. Most of us take great pride in our parental competence or understanding of same. Finally, we often think we have control over the children, at least in the short run.

I won't belabor the "technical benefits" of parenthood, but they are many, including being in charge. But just like in a leadership role, in order to get the most out of this parental relationship, ultimately we have to recognize that the parenting style that worked best in the earlier years may actually hinder our success and the development of the children in the later years. We truly have to give up on some of the control and allow the children to grow and begin making their own decisions and accepting their own consequences. To be the most successful as parents, we literally need to move from details to big picture and from supervising to partnering. Remember, when your children make the most important decisions in their lives, most likely you will not be there. You must prepare them for these crucial moments.

It is very important to remember that our children have grown up in different times and with different experiences. About one year ago, I heard a story about Gabriel, our teenage granddaughter by heart (a grandchild of some good friends). Gab's mother, Anne, asked Gab to call her great-grandmother in New Jersey and wish her a happy ninety plus birthday. Gab left the room to make the call but returned in just a couple of minutes. Anne said, "Well, you could have talked with her a little longer." Gab responded, "No, Mom, you don't understand. I called her several times, but I kept getting this funny sound." Great-grandma did not have an answering machine, and Gab had never heard a busy signal on a telephone.

We had a similar experience with our granddaughter Abby. she was trying out for a local theater production of *Fiddler on the Roof.* We owned a VHS version of the *Fiddler on the Roof* movie, and we all sat down to watch it with her. When the movie ended, Jennifer got up and started to rewind the VHS tape. Abby asked what Jennifer was doing. She had never had to rewind anything. She had never seen the Be Kind—Rewind notes from the video store.

As to the role of partner, I will discuss a concept I call being the senior partner in a relationship under the "Be Situational" chapter. Suffice to say for now, if you choose to take on the senior partner role, you too will have to give up some things you might value to get the benefits desired.

Begin Each Circumstance Anew—Summary

Merry Browne, author of many books, wrote,

> Preconceived notions are the locks on the door to wisdom.

Here is the story of the woman preparing a special meal for her family. Every year, she bakes a ham for Thanksgiving dinner. Before she puts it in the roasting pan, she cuts both ends off the ham. One year, her young daughter asks why she does this. She tells her daughter that this is just the way it's done; her mother did it this way, as did her mother before her. Not being satisfied with this answer, the little girl approaches her great-grandmother with the same question. "Well," the elderly woman replies, "I had to cut the ends off the ham so it would fit into the only roasting pan I had, which was very small."

By never beginning anew, there was a lot of good ham wasted over the years! In order to be the best leader, parent, and/or partner we must be willing to balance calling on our past experiences and assessing each new circumstance we encounter anew. We must make a conscious decision to avoid stereotyping and preconceived negative biases. We must make the essential transition from technical person to leader and from controlling, autocratic parent to a parent leader.

By the way, as mentioned earlier, the correct answer to the number of Fs quiz from the beginning of this chapter is six. I did this exercise many years ago for the Kansas City Actuaries Club. I had the group read the sentence one time, then asked them to count the number of Fs in the sentence. I had the usual result—most only saw three, or at most four, Fs. Very few saw all six Fs. When I asked them to look one more time and be sure to consider the word *of*, one of them said aloud, "Well, those are the three that I had!" I've always been pretty sure that guy was pulling my leg, but maybe not. After all, actuaries are very technical in nature.

Why do you think most people miss the F in each use of the word *of*? One common reason is that we tend to overlook the small things. Have you ever gotten into trouble in your personal relationships when you overlooked what you thought was a small thing that was not so small to the other person? If you've been married more than two months, I'm pretty sure you have. Is counting the Fs in the word a small thing given the assignment? Another reason most miss all six Fs the first time directly relates to a preconceived idea that for many goes back to being "hooked on phonics." Various people perceive the word *of* phonetically as "ov". In this case, a preconceived idea misleads us. We should have begun anew. And finally, this little exercise reinforces the idea that we already have the tools to address our needs, if we only use the tools we have.

In case you are still having trouble finding all six Fs, I have highlighted and underscored the six Fs below.

<u>F</u>INISHED <u>F</u>ILES ARE THE RE-
SULT O<u>F</u> YEARS O<u>F</u> SCIENTI<u>F</u>-
IC STUDY COMBINED WITH THE
EXPERIENCE O<u>F</u> MANY YEARS.

Be Situational

The *S* in the BASIC strategy stands for *situational*. Meaning when using these strategies, we must also take into account the specifics of each unique situation.

Following are the key concepts of being situational:

- Be the senior partner in a relationship.
- Values and significant emotional events impact behavior.
- Different frames of reference cause different reactions.
- There are no absolutes—flexibility is a sign of maturity.
- People often need your care most when they deserve it the least.

Be the Senior Partner in a Relationship

To be effective leaders, partners, and parents, we must be able to adapt to the needs of the others in our lives. I define the senior partner as the one in the relationship who is most able and willing to take ultimate responsibility for the best possible ongoing relationship. In a supervisor and employee relationship, it is usually pretty clear who is formally in charge, but the supervisor isn't always what I would call the senior partner, usually but not always. In the early years of a parent and child relationship, the parent is by default the senior partner, but this can change, and in some cases, the child becomes the senior partner as the parent and child age. The definition and meaning of the senior partner in a marriage or another long-term partnership is much less obvious. By senior partner I don't mean the one who is dominant, but rather, I mean the one in the relationship who is willing and able to take ultimate responsibility for the best possible ongoing relationship. I believe the more one attempts and succeeds in implementing these BASIC strategies, the closer he or she is to functioning as the senior partner in a marriage or any long-term partnership.

Steven Spielberg, the director of *Jaws, Raiders of the Lost Ark, ET, Jurassic Park, Schindler's List, Saving Private Ryan, Lincoln, War Horse,* and many other movies, is reported to have once said,

> Every actor needs a different director at different times—
> my job is to be that director.

More important than the source of the quote is a realization of the fact that

- every employee needs a different leader at different times. It is the senior partner's job to be situational and flexible enough to be that needed leader;
- every partner needs a different partner at different times. It is the senior partner's job to be situational and flexible enough to be that needed partner;
- every child, at different times, needs a different parent. It is the senior partner's job to be situational and flexible enough to be that needed parent.

Conditions and circumstances change, and people are different. We must be flexible and situational to have the best possible relationships.

Also, keep in mind that periods of change directly affect relationships. A personal example has to do with a Christmas gift from long ago. I normally place my wallet in my left side back pocket. This particular Christmas, Janis gave me a new pair of pants that only had one back pocket—and on the right side. I have a habit of periodically tapping my back left pocket to make sure my wallet is still there. When I wore these pants, I found myself tapping my left buttock and thinking, *Where is my wallet?* Then I would feel the right buttock and think, *What's that?* To further complicate the change (and to illustrate how long ago this was), these new Christmas pants also did not have a fly. Yes, change can be disruptive. For most, including me in this instance, even a slight physical change can cause discomfort or resistance. What does this imply for more substantial physical changes?

Values and Significant Emotional Events Impact Behavior

Consider reviewing the discussion of values and behavior under the first *B*—understanding behavior. Remember that we need to understand people's value systems. A value is something a person is willing to make a sacrifice for. In my case, getting my bachelor's degree at night school was worth the sacrifice of personal time because I valued that accomplishment. It is important to know your own value system and, as much as you can, the value systems of the other people in your life because value systems impact behavior.

Review the discussion of Morris Massey's theory on *What You Are Is Where You Were When*. In essence, his theory is that the time you were born and raised impacts your values. When I was growing up, my parents and most of their peers had been raised in the Great Depression and thus were very frugal and money conscious. People in my and later generations didn't have these same base values. Things came easier for us.

Remember also the discussion of how our value systems can change as we go through life, what Massey calls significant emotional events (SEEs). A very SEE in my life was the birth of our granddaughter, Abigail Marie Walker. My younger brother, Jon, had four grandchildren before Abby was born. I remember many times him telling me how special it was to be a grandparent. I also remember telling him that I was a well-read, caring guy and that I certainly understood and appreciated the special feelings for grandchildren. Well, I had no idea of how special having a grandchild is. Grandchildren are SEEs. They reintroduce you to the world.

All the members of my immediate family are Disney freaks. We go to

Disney World often, usually once a year. I remember seeing other families there with infants and very small toddlers and telling my family we will never do that! I often said, "We will wait until our grandkids are at least eight to ten years old before we take them to Disney World." Abby was less

than two when we first took her to Disney World. I have often said of that first trip with Abby that she won't remember it, but I will never forget it. It was so wonderful seeing this very familiar place through her eyes.

The legendary comedian Bill Cosby says that grandchildren are your reward for not having killed your own children. He has a wonderful routine on the relationship between grandparents and grandchildren. He says of his own parents and how they treat his children, their grandchildren,

"Who are these people? These are not the people that raised me!"

He further explains the reason that grandparents and grandchildren get along so well: "They have a common enemy—me!"

Do you have or have you had a teenager in the house? Have they or did they go through the hormone explosion? This was the case when I accused my daughter Jennifer of going to sleep one night as Cinderella and awakening as Godzilla.

Different Frames of Reference Cause Different Reactions

When considering particular situations you encounter, keep in mind that your situation or position in life can cause different frames of reference. So different frames of reference cause different reactions to situations. Consider the following example:

Three people are standing on a street corner and simultaneously observe a serious auto accident. One of the three is a nurse. What do you think the nurse will think of first after observing this accident? Most people answer along the lines of pain, suffering, need for assistance, etc. A second witness to the accident is a police officer. What are the police officer's first thoughts? Most mention fault (certainly from my insurance audiences), followed by such things as paperwork and court time. Now the third person to witness this same automobile accident is the owner of an automobile body repair shop. What are this businessperson's first thoughts? Most say dollars, sales, or revenue. This simple story illustrates how three different people seeing the same event can have three different first reactions to that same event based on their different frames of reference. We all come to our relationships from many different backgrounds and experiences, which require us to try to understand the other person's frame of reference and be as cognizant of their situation as possible. Remember, be situational when possible.

There Are No Absolutes—
Flexibility Is a Sign of Maturity

Senator Everett Dirksen, leader of Senate Republicans from 1959 to 1969, once said,

> I am a man of fixed and unbending principles,
> the first of which is to be flexible at all times.

When it comes to supervising, parenting, being a loving partner, there is no magic bullet. What works today or tomorrow may not work with the same person next week. The challenge is to make yourself aware of a broad spectrum of ideas from which you can select the right strategy/response (response, not reaction!). The most success will come from choosing a style or response depending on the context of the situation and the developmental maturity of the other person. Where possible and practical, choose based more on the needs of the other person rather than your own needs. This is choosing to be the senior partner. Don't allow yourself to be locked into always being a drill sergeant, or even always a coach, enabler, or even mentor. Learn to respect the differences in others. Consider all the variables. Any relationship style can be appropriate under certain circumstances depending on the variables. Consider all the mind-sets within yourself, the other people, and the environment in which you are all operating.

Effective people are flexible. Flexibility is truly a highlight of maturity. We often tend to be more flexible with people we know less than we are with the people we know best. We should be as flexible with our spouse and children as we are with the people in the office. For best results, remember, the burden of adaptation or flexibility is on the senior partner.

People Often Need Care Most When
They Deserve It the Least

This one last point on this subject is so very important. It is especially true in the parent role. My experience has taught me several times that *people often need our flexibility, understanding, and care most when they deserve it the least*. We are all human, and we all make mistakes. The senior partner in a positive relationship looks at these matters very objectively and bends over backward to be flexible, sometimes when the other person deserves it the least.

Most parents at some time will have to deal with some form of rebellion by their children. The natural reaction of the parent is to exercise their authority by demanding respect and compliance. The usual response by the child is more resistance since, as we learned in basic physics, force creates resistance. Then the child's resistance often leads to more or accelerated threats by the parent and more poor responses by the child and eventually to a wider gap in the relationship. Avoiding all rebellions is not possible as this is part of growing up. However, we can limit the damage by applying some of the BASIC strategies. First and foremost, decide to be the senior partner and be situational. Work to understand the underlying reasons for the behavior. Keep your balance by not stressing out and overreacting. Minimize the arguing and avoid judging. Try to see the situation from the child's frame of reference. Take this as an opportunity to better communicate. Most of all, use this as a time for reinforcement of your loving care. Times of rebellion, no matter how small or large, are best handled by care, love, and kindness. I have always tried to let my child and grandchild know that "no matter what you do, no matter what you say, I will always love you."

There is an old Swedish proverb that expresses the key idea of this section with focus on the child: "Love me when I least deserve it, because that is when I really need it."

The same BASIC principles can apply when faced with some form of rebellion in the leadership and partner roles.

Be Situational—Summary

Being situational involves a willingness to be flexible when the circumstances call for a different course of action. Being willing to take on the role of the senior partner and to demonstrate flexibility in your relationships will result in happier and more constructive relationships with most everyone. As you approach each interaction, keep in mind circumstances that could be influencing the other person. This includes their value systems and frame of reference. Remember, the most success will come from choosing a style or response depending on the context of the situation and the developmental maturity of the other person.

Consider the following advice from George Washington Carver:

> How far you go in life depends on your being tender with the young,
> compassionate with the aged,
> sympathetic with the striving and
> tolerant of the weak and strong.
> Because someday in your life you will have been all of these.

Watch the *I*

The *I* in the BASIC strategy represents the need to balance the value of a high level of self-confidence with the dangers and inherent limitations of becoming too focused on oneself.

Following are the key concepts of watching the *I*:

- Build a strong and positive but balanced self-image.
- There is no *I* in teamwork.
- Build relationships—network.
- Embrace the big picture.
- Recognize political and power forces.
- Delegate at work and at home.

Build a Strong and Positive but Balanced Self-Image

Finding the right balance between a strong, positive self-image and letting your ego run amok is a real key in the successful implementation of the BASIC strategy.

A significant part of this theory revolves around the power of the thoughts we have about ourselves. The subconscious mind is a powerful force in our lives. Unfortunately, the subconscious mind doesn't know what is real and what is not real. Thus, if you are thinking bad things about yourself, your mind will carry these negative thoughts forward as though they are real, regardless of whether they are fact-based or not. I like the work of Lee J. Colan in *Orchestrating Attitude* wherein he discusses the relationship between our thoughts and our ultimate effectiveness. Our thoughts directly influence our beliefs. Our beliefs directly influence the words we choose to speak to others and to ourselves. Our chosen words reflect our commitments, which influence our actions. Our actions influence the results we achieve.

If we go through life with a negative self-image, our chances for better BASIC relationships are significantly reduced. An old saying is that if you think you are stupid, it won't take you long to prove it. A key to a positive self-image is how we talk to ourselves and how we talk to others. Mastering how we talk with ourselves is a big challenge.

A totally self-centered person (especially a negative self-centered person) will have less success in developing positive relationships with others. We must also keep in mind the difference between being self-centered and taking care of yourself. You must take care of yourself first. It is the same as when the airline flight attendants advise parents in the event of an emergency to put their oxygen masks on first and then help their child or, as one said on a recent flight, the person next to you that is acting like a child.

I like the story of the greatest hitter in the world. It seems there was this young man (might have been me!) who was practicing hitting a baseball out of his hand in the backyard. Hitting the baseball out of our hands is what we did as kids when there was no one else around to play ball. It involves tossing the ball in the air, clutching the bat, and hitting the ball as it comes back down toward the earth. It seems this particular young man was full of self-confidence, and as he tossed the ball up in the air, he shouted, "I am the greatest hitter in the world" and then he swung mightily—and missed. Not deterred, he picked up the ball and again tossed it in the air while declaring once again, "I am the greatest hitter in the world." He swung mightily, but once again, he missed. Full of self-confidence he picked the ball up once more, tossed it into the air a third time, and once again declared, "I am the greatest hitter in the world." But unfortunately, swinging as hard as he could, he missed the ball once again. He thought for a moment, picked up the ball once more, tossed it into the air, and in an even louder voice shouted, "I am the greatest *pitcher* in the world."

There Is No I in Teamwork

Even though several recent books claim there really is an I in team or teamwork, my point here is to simply remember that people will work much better *with* you than *for* you.

Build Relationships—Network

In all our roles in life, it pays to build up other people's knowledge of us. There have been many books written on the value of networking in a leadership role. Whether we call it networking or not, we do it all the time by helping each other, meeting other people, working on committees, etc. The advantages of networking, in whatever form, include increasing the chances of being successful and achieving your goals by connecting with others who can provide guidance and support as and when needed. Networking provides access to needed information and opportunities and allows you to sharpen your interpersonal skills. Networking is also very important when you change jobs, either voluntarily or not.

It is important to realize that the benefits you receive by networking in a leadership role have the same positive results when networking in your role as a partner or parent. Establishing trusting relationships with other parents can provide the opportunity for lots of good and timely information sharing. It is also my experience that positive networking with others helps keep a partnership relationship healthy.

Embrace the Big Picture

One of the biggest challenges in any relationship is to keep the big picture in focus, particularly in hard times. Don't allow yourself to be distracted from your ultimate goals and desires by little and less important events that happen along the way.

Recognize Political and Power Forces

Marilyn Moats Kennedy, a business author and keynote speaker, in her book *Office Politics* says, "Office politics is today what sex was to the Victorians—interesting, sometimes fun, but nothing anyone with the least claim to a proper upbringing would dare talk about in public."

Politics is not necessarily a bad thing. Politics, or being political, is simply obtaining support for the policy directions you wish to pursue. It is paving the way to achievement with goodwill. You should accept politics as the necessary formation of coalitions to get things done in organizations, families, and other relationships. Recognize that politics can be a positive force and can serve purposes with which you are in sympathy.

All organizations and most personal relationships are influenced by political and power forces. Even a two-person lemonade stand is affected by these powerful forces. Although political and power forces are easier to detect in the leadership role, they also exist in the personal roles as well. In a leadership role, it is important to recognize that all organizational politics are not bad. In truth, politics in an organization represents how things really get done. This is not to say that there are not bad actors who may use the natural political system for bad purposes. However, you should not dismiss the whole political ecosystem because of some bad actors. We don't dismiss driving our cars because some people are bad drivers or use cars for bad purposes.

The positive use of politics in an organization may involve asking for support, expecting to be called on by others for your support, allowing others to have your ideas, and oftentimes getting out and socializing with others in the organization.

I have often told the story of how I used politics to obtain support for a new system I wanted to pursue while at Frankona. At the time (late '80s) voice mail was just becoming a popular productivity tool in the American workplace. I had talked with many vendors and developed a very strong case for the efficiency and cost savings and better customer service that could be obtained by implementing a voice mail system. Despite my excellent presentation, my proposal was rejected as "too far out there."

I decided to use some politics to help me get this new "radical" idea approved. At the time, our sales staff traveled quite a bit. They were in sales calls all day, and the only way to get their new messages was to check in with their secretary. (For younger readers, go to http:// en.wikipedia.org/wiki/Secretary to learn what a secretary is!)

Since at this time the sales team did not have cell phones or e-mail, the only way they could get their new messages was to talk with their secretary. I had heard that, many times, by the time they ended their meetings, the secretary had gone home for the day. Therefore the messages would be at least delayed by one day. I met quietly with each of the sales persons and explained to them how having voice mail would allow them to check on their own messages (by using a pay phone to call in and get their messages!). I also pointed out that they could actually check their messages anytime during the day and that they would hear the caller's actual message, tone, etc., rather than having the secretary transcribe and interpret the call.

To make a long story short, the sales people liked the voice mail idea and began asking the sales management team for voice mail. Eventually the voice mail proposal came back up the leadership chain and this time was approved. This process of asking for support, and allowing others to have my idea, is a good example of using politics on a positive basis to get something that was ultimately good for the organization.

There can be many opportunities to use the same power of politics in our partner and parental roles. As a parent, I was never above the idea of letting Jennifer think that it was her idea to break off a relationship with a certain young man. I don't see anything positive that could come out of specifically mentioning and publishing examples of using politics in my marriage partner relationship. However, I'm sure most readers can remember a few personal opportunities to use positive politics in their partner relationship.

It is also important in a leadership role to recognize and work within the power structure that exists in an organization. Power exists in many forms in most organizations:

- Representative power, which is that vested in supervisors.
- Expertise power, which is granted to persons respected for their formal training and knowledge, such as doctors, lawyers, teachers, etc.
- Esteem power, which is granted because others like and respect the person.
- Positional power, which is associated with a title or position, such as vice presidents in a bank.
- Reward power, which is granted to those who have control of the goodies.
- Power through fear.
- Power through chance.

Understanding and judicious use of these powers, whether yours or someone else's, can be very instrumental in your ultimate organizational success.

While power is more fluid in the partner and parental roles, one can easily see that as a parent you certainly have elements of all the power types. The definition and use of power is less clear and more dangerous in the partner role.

Delegate at Work and Home

Bill Marriott Sr., founder of the Marriott Hotel chain, offered the following:

> Don't do anything that someone else can do for you.

Effective delegation is a major key to successful leadership and relationship building. A guiding principle first taught to me in my years at General American is that *every job should be done at the lowest economic level consistent with the quality required.*

Delegation is also an important part of successful development of employees and even of children as we perform the parental role. I have also seen delegation be a big part of successful partnership role playing (such as in division of the household duties).

Not delegating properly is one of our biggest time wasters. So if delegation is so crucial to relationship success, why don't people delegate more or better?

Probably the most common reason is the often false belief that nobody can do it better. We often feel that only we can do the job with the level of care and expertise needed. This attitude is very limiting and negates the increased productivity that is gained when we are able to leverage the work of many.

A second common reason is a feeling of insecurity—a fear of losing control, of competition from associates, or a lack of confidence in the other persons.

A third common reason for not delegating is that it takes time. Like money, you must invest time to save time. Think of the example of teaching your children to tie their shoes. While it does take time initially, there is a much larger payoff in time savings down the road.

The final common reason for not delegating is just simply habit. We continue to avoid delegating because we have always done the work ourselves. It just feels more comfortable.

Not delegating prevents others from using their skills and abilities, stifles their creativity, and misuses time of both parties.

A strong, problem solving, independent-achievement-oriented desire to do things ourselves can make delegation even more difficult. Sound familiar? Delegation is particularly difficult for technical people.

A personal example for me has to do with our home maintenance. We live in a nice stand-alone home in Overland Park, Kansas, a suburb of Kansas City. Although we are surrounded by maintenance-provided neighborhoods, our home is in a traditional do-it-yourself neighborhood. My wife, Janis, says, however, that we really live in a maintenance-provided home—it is just that the maintenance is provided by a whole group of different workers that she has to hire. You see, my philosophy is to calculate an hourly billing rate for chores around the home that I don't like to do (which by the way is most of them!). I then compare my mythical personal hourly rate with the costs of having someone else do it. I also take into account the high probability of a better quality job and the benefit of my doing something more enjoyable with the time. My pseudo personal hourly billing rate is pretty high when it comes to doing maintenance work around the house, especially when you consider the quality of my work. My rate is especially high for plumbing, and as long as the tradesmen work for a lower hourly rate (which they almost always do), I delegate these duties to them.

I mentioned some concerns about the quality of my handyman work. I think this goes all the way back to my elementary school days. As part of the seventh-grade curriculum, we were bussed off to O'Fallon Technical School once a week for what was called manual arts. The purpose of these classes was to surface any latent craftsman-type skills. Suffice it to say, I had no such latent skills. This became abundantly clear to me one day toward the end of the "torture." The final class project was to create a cutting board, similar to the one pictured here. My final version did not look much like this picture. In fact, when I touched one side, it would wobble for a long time. My classmate  Dave Edgar was a master at manual arts, and his cutting board was both beautiful and functional. When it came time for Mr. Furner to grade our final project, I arranged with Dave to trade boards. We were lined up in alphabetical order, and so Dave's board was reviewed first and he was given an A grade. He then quickly, and without detection, passed his board back to me. I presented the same board to Mr. Furmer as my project. I received a C on the same board! Not only did this experience teach me that cheating was wrong but it also discouraged any further development of my manual skills. The final irony is that when I took an aptitude test just before my high school graduation, the recommendation was that I be a sheet metal worker! I'm sure glad I did not follow that recommendation.

Watch the *I*—Summary

To be the most effective leader, partner, and parent possible, you must find the proper balance between having a strong positive self-image and not allowing yourself to become too egotistic—at the same time, keeping your eye on the big picture. It is also very important that you realize the impact of others through networking. Also, recognize the political and power forces that impact you and all the people in your life. An important key to your personal productivity in all your roles is learning to delegate.

Improve Communication

As noted earlier, there are three *C*s in the BASIC strategy. They are communication, care, and common sense.

The first C represents improving communication. Virginia Satir, a family therapy pioneer, writes, "Communication is to personal health, satisfactory interpersonal relationships, and productivity as breathing is to life." Effective communication can be both taught and learned. We were not born with the way we communicate. We learned it, mostly through modeling.

Communication, or lack of same, is often the sand in our relationships. Think back to the last significant problem you had in one of your relationships. In most cases, poor communication contributes to the problem.

- More than 75 percent of our waking hours are spent in some form of communication.
- Peter Drucker said 60 percent of all management problems are communications related.
- Criminologists say 90 percent of all criminals have difficulty communicating effectively.
- A leading marriage counselor says at least 50 percent of all divorces result from a breakdown in communication between spouses.
- Louis D. Brandeis, an American lawyer and associate justice on the Supreme Court of the United States from 1916 to 1939, said, "Nine-tenths of the serious controversies which arise in life result from misunderstandings."

Communication is hard, and the lack of proper communication threatens all relationships.

Following are the key concepts of improving communication:

- Practice effective listening. Listening must be learned and consciously activated.
- Pick your words carefully.
- Remember, all of us are imperfect communicators.

Practice Effective Listening

A couple of years ago at the end of the Father's Day Mass, the priest asked all the fathers to stand to receive a special blessing. I watched painfully as the lady sitting across from me rose to her feet. It was apparent she wasn't effectively listening to the priest, and it resulted in her being embarrassed. Effective listening must be learned and consciously activated.

Various studies have reported that our methods of communicating by type break down as something like the following:

- Nine percent by writing
- Sixteen percent by reading
- Thirty percent by speaking
- Forty-five percent by listening

Listening is the most common component of communication, and yet, we have very little formal training in effective listening. Our ears may be the most underused relationship tool we have, and our mouths may be our most overused relationship tool.

Effective listening is a contest between concentration and preoccupation. The average person speaks between 125 and 200 words per minute. Our brains have the capacity to accept at least 450 words per minute. So what happens during the gap? If we are not disciplined, the brain takes little side trips to fill the gaps (day dreaming). To listen effectively, we must be radically present in the moment.

We need to understand the difference between hearing (a biological activity that can't be helped unless there is organ or brain damage) and listening (a psychological process that must be learned and consciously activated). You are never in deeper trouble in a relationship than when you think you are listening and all you are really doing is hearing. The true test of listening is being able to repeat what was said in your own words and to have it confirmed by the other person.

Active listening involves understanding and compassion. Show that you are interested by maintaining eye contact, nodding, smiling, etc. Avoid interrupting the other person. Allow the other person to finish, and avoid formulating your response while the other person is talking.

Pick Your Words Carefully

Being an effective listener is complicated by what I call the problem of words. Consider this question: do words *give* a meaning or *get* a meaning? Let's play a word association game. What comes to mind if I offer the word *egg*? Most likely things like breakfast, bacon, cholesterol, etc., come to mind. Now let's do the same thing with the word avgo. What do you think of when I say avgo? I imagine not much. You see, avgo is the Greek word for egg. Therefore, understand that *it is our frame of reference that gives words meaning*. Words themselves cannot give or have meaning.

So what's the problem? Well, depending on how we count and define words, one source indicates there are well over six hundred thousand words in the English language. We add more than one thousand new words each year. The average person commands between thirty thousand and sixty thousand words. More than five thousand words have significant multiple meanings, and between three thousand and four thousand words are in common usage. The five hundred most commonly used words have more than fourteen thousand different definitions.

All this to say that coding and decoding our communications through all this is difficult. We must constantly clarify, restate, and get and give feedback to confirm the meaning of our communications. It can often be dangerous to assume that the other party has gotten the correct message.

I spent most of my adult working career in the insurance and training industry. Many insurance customers have experienced the confusion of traffic accidents and have had to summarize correctly what happened in a few words on an insurance claim form. The following quotes were taken from those forms and were eventually published in the *Toronto Sun* newspaper:

- "I was on my way to the doctor's with rear end trouble when my universal joint gave way causing me to have an accident."
- "I pulled away from the side of the road, glanced at my mother-in-law, and headed over the embankment."
- "I was sure the old fellow would never make it to the other side of the street when I struck him."
- "The telephone pole was approaching fast. I attempted to swerve out of its way, when it struck the front of my car."

Communication errors are not just an insurance problem. Here are a couple more examples of miscommunication in real letters and applications for aid or assistance: (Note: I'm not making fun of the persons or their needs, only the choice of words resulting in failed communication.)

- "My husband got his project cut off two weeks ago. I haven't had any relief since."
- "I want money as soon as possible. I have been in bed with the doctor for two weeks, and he doesn't do me any good. If things don't improve, I will have to send for another doctor."

Professionals are often challenged as well. Here are some actual newspaper headlines:

- "Include Your Children When Baking Cookies"
- "Plane Too Close to Ground, Crash Probe Told"
- "Typhoon Rips Through Cemetery, Hundreds Dead"
- "Local High School Dropouts Cut in Half"
- "Police Begin Campaign to Run Down Jaywalkers"
- "Prostitutes Appeal to Pope"
- "Something Went Wrong in Jet Crash, Experts Say"
- "Teacher Strikes Idle Kids"
- "If Strike Isn't Settled Quickly, It Will Last A While"
- "Kids Make Nutritious Snacks"

My brother, Jon, tells a story about his five-year-old granddaughter picking the wrong words at the wrong time. They were attending a funeral service for Jon's wife's grandmother. The granddaughter had recently been watching *The Wizard of Oz* videotape (yes, before DVDs!) and suddenly, in a quiet part of the funeral service, blurted out a favorite song phrase from the movie: "Ding dong the witch is dead." Truly the wrong words at the wrong time.

Finally, my friend and colleague Cary Phillips tells the story of his then young daughter coming out of school one day, all excited about the day's events. When Cary asked what happened, his young daughter explained that one of the teachers had overheated some popcorn in the microwave and that there was a lot of smoke in the

teacher's lounge. Cary asked, "Did the smoke alarm go off?" His daughter gave him a puzzled look and said, "No, Dad, the smoke alarm went *on*. Why would it go *off*?" Cary's astute reply was, "I don't know why I would ask if it went *off*." A good example of a communication error.

Remember, All of Us Are Imperfect Communicators

All of us are imperfect communicators, but some of us are further from perfection than others. So even if you are perfect, you will have problems since you will have to deal with the rest of us who are imperfect.

Here is an example of how punctuation and emphasis can lead to imperfect communications. Read the following sentence aloud:

Woman without her man is nothing.

Most men will read this sentence with the following emphasis and punctuation:

Woman, *without her man*, is nothing.

Most women, however, will read this sentence with the following emphasis and punctuation:

Woman, *without her*, man is nothing.

As illustrated above, with a small change in punctuation or emphasis, a totally different meaning can come from the same six words. Recently, I was writing out this exercise on a whiteboard and got the words *her* and *man* a little too close to each other, causing an attendee to read the sentence as follows:

Woman, without *herman*, is nothing.

Everyone wanted to meet Herman.

Also, be aware that noise and other distractions, as well as speaking and hearing mismatches, can be additional barriers to effective communication. An example of a speaking and hearing mismatch occurred when I was chairman of the board of directors of the Insurance

Accounting and Systems Association. One of my fellow board members was an elderly gentleman from Boston, Massachusetts, and another was a classic southern lady from Durham, North Carolina. Often they had trouble understanding each other. At times, I had to translate.

Improve Communication—Summary

As Ralph Waldo Emerson once said, "It is a luxury to be understood." Good communications are essential to the optimal implementation of the BASIC strategy. One of the greatest compliments you can pay to others in your life is to listen to them with your full attention. Practice effective listening skills in all your relationships. Pick your words carefully, and ask for affirmation of key points when necessary.

A now funny story on my failure to communicate happened in 1980 when we were in the process of moving from St. Louis to Kansas City. It was a stressful span of time when we owned two houses, one in Kansas City where I lived while working at my new job and one in St. Louis that Janis and the girls continued to occupy until we could sell it. We had a bridge loan so we could pay the mortgage on each house, and the interest rates at that time were very high. Finally, we received a bona fide offer for the St. Louis house, and since I was in Kansas City, I needed to send a telegram to the realtor in St. Louis agreeing to the buyers' offer. Some of you are thinking, what is a telegram or at least why a telegram? Well, it was 1980, and we did not have the Internet or e-mail and not many had a fax machine. So the most practical and timely way to get my acceptance of the offer documented was to call Western Union and send a telegram. The complication at that moment though was that I had two wisdom teeth removed that day, and my mouth was full of blood-soaked cotton. When I called Western Union and mumbled, "I need to send a telegram," the operator hung up on me, most likely thinking I was either drunk or playing a practical joke. I tried a second time to call and again the operator hung up on me. On the third call, I started with a plea, "Please don't hang up on me!" With a little patience and understanding on that particular Western Union operator's part, I was able to get my message through to her with my formal agreement, and thus the deal did close. The moral here is that communication is hard, even when all the necessary parts are working properly, but it can be even harder when various obstacles are placed in our way.

Handle People with Care

The second *C* brings the important concept of *care* into the BASIC strategy.

Following are the key concepts of handling people with care:

- We get back from people what we give them.
- People don't care how much you know until they know how much you care.
- When the student is ready, the teacher arrives.
- Be tough on results but tender on people.
- Attack the problem, not the person.

We Get Back from People What We Give Them

As mentioned in earlier chapters, the BASIC strategy came out of my work helping to develop a course on making the transition from a technical role to a leadership role. Another interesting aspect to come out of developing and facilitating this course is a pretty comprehensive list of the characteristics of the best and worst leaders. One of the attendees described a worst leader as someone who lights up the room when they leave.

Characteristics of the best leaders included the following:

- Honest
- Competent
- Visionary
- Inspiring
- Intelligent
- Fair-minded
- Broad-minded
- Straight forward
- Imaginative

- Dependable
- Confident
- Risk taker
- Action oriented
- Adaptable
- Enthusiastic
- Efficient
- Good communicator
- People oriented
- Optimistic
- Provides direction/mission
- Good teacher
- Problem solver
- Supportive

Characteristics of the worst leaders included the following:

- None of the "best" characteristics
- Distant and cold
- Autocratic
- Out for him or herself
- Lazy/unmotivated
- Uncertain about job
- Avoids conflict
- Resists change
- Can't handle stress
- Impatient
- Poor time manager
- Poor communicator
- Not objective
- Too emotional
- Biased
- Poor listener

In discussions with several attendees, most agreed that many of the best leader characteristics imply a required level of care for others. So conversely, many of the worst leader characteristics imply a lack of caring.

One of the major reasons leaders fail is their insensitivity to others. They are often unable to understand things from other people's perspectives. We get back from people what we give them. Think back to the people who had a strong, positive influence on you. Most likely you will realize they were people who really cared about you. A teacher, a special friend, a business associate—someone who was really interested and supportive, someone who really cared about and for you.

A great example of the value of care occurs in one of my favorite episodes from *The Wonder Years* television series that ran on ABC from 1988 through 1993. The episode entitled "Good-bye" revolves around the relationship between Kevin Arnold and his math teacher, Mr. Collins. Mr. Collins pushes Kevin to succeed in math. Kevin becomes antagonistic toward his teacher when he feels Collins is ignoring him, only to become regretful when tragedy befalls Mr. Collins.

Following is a summary of the plot as extracted in part from Wikipedia.[5]

> Kevin Arnold (Fred Savage) is averaging a "respectable" C in Mr. Collins' math class. Despite his best efforts, Kevin can only muster average 'C' grades. Kevin is mostly content with this, reasoning to himself that he is trying his best. However, Kevin becomes curious when he sees that his best friend Paul received a note from Mr. Collins on his math paper. Kevin stops to talk with Mr. Collins regarding his progress in the class, expecting Collins to be impressed with his C grades. When Mr. Collins doesn't reciprocate Kevin's enthusiasm for his C grades, Kevin begins to wonder why. Kevin stops Mr. Collins in the courtyard who explains that he (Mr. Collins) does not believe Kevin is achieving his potential in the class. Mr. Collins begins to personally tutor Kevin, and the two develop a unique bond in the class.
>
> After several tutoring sessions in preparation for the midterm, one afternoon, Mr. Collins suddenly tells Kevin that he would not be able to help Kevin with his math anymore

---

[5]   "Good-bye," *The Wonder Years, Wikipedia, the free encyclopedia,* <u>accessed January 14, 2014,</u> http://en.wikipedia.org/wiki/Good-bye_(The_Wonder_Years)

due to other appointments. Kevin takes this harshly, saying, "We had a deal," to which Collins replies that he is just Kevin's math teacher. Feeling betrayed, Kevin purposefully flunks the midterm examination, writing "who cares" and "???" in response to the questions, which disturbs Mr. Collins greatly. Kevin drops his test off and rushes out of the class, to Collins calling "Kevin!" which Kevin ignores. Later, Kevin regrets his decision to flunk the test, as the weekend progresses.

Kevin returns on Monday, and asks to see Mr. Collins in the teachers' lounge to apologize for his behavior. Mr. DiPerna surprises Kevin at the door and pulls him aside, explaining that Mr. Collins had died over the weekend from a heart condition, something he was suffering from for a long time. DiPerna apologizes for telling Kevin this news prior to a school-wide announcement, and informs Kevin that he will be taking over the class.

Kevin is distraught at this news, and sincerely regrets his decision to scorn Mr. Collins in such a way. A week later, Kevin and Paul are eating lunch in the cafe and one of Kevin's friends pokes fun at Kevin and Paul. Kevin flicks Jell-O on his friend, and DiPerna asks to see Kevin after school.

DiPerna informs Kevin that Mr. Collins had "lost" his exam and asks if Kevin has any ideas what to do about it. Kevin says he doesn't have any ideas, and DiPerna says, "Well, Mr. Collins did," and reveals an uncompleted test that Collins wrote 'Kevin Arnold' at the top of it. Kevin realizes that Mr. Collins had posthumously given him a second chance to prove himself, and sees this as his opportunity to make amends with him, and proceeds to ace the exam, telling DiPerna, "You don't have to grade it, it's an A." As Kevin leaves the classroom, he looks back at Collins' old desk, and sees a vision of Collins in the chair with a look of approval on his face, and says out loud, "Good job, Mr. Collins." The camera dims as Kevin walks out of the building and several black and white slides of Collins in the yearbook are shown as the closing music plays.

For me, this episode beautifully represents the power of care. People like the fictional Mr. Collins exist in all our lives. Sometimes we fail to notice them or appreciate them. We also have the ability to influence other people in our life by using the power of care.

Other people will sense your level of care and understanding and will develop a stronger bond with you as they sense your level of care. Caring for people is worthy in building yourself, but it also has amazing power in building others as well.

People Don't Care How Much You Know

I have seen the following statement *"People don't care how much you know, until they know how much you care"* attributed to different people, ranging from John Maxwell to Martin Luther King. The source isn't nearly as important as the inherent message of how important caring is in any relationship. When people care about you and believe you care about them, they are much more likely to believe in you, support you, and learn from you.

A person who cares for others can most positively influence others. A person with influence nurtures, listens, understands, connects, and empowers other people. A truly caring person also reeks of integrity.

The impact of care is difficult to test or show in tangible ways. Most often, we see the impact of care in an observable phenomenon rather than a testable phenomenon. Care can often be communicated with a simple incidental touch. Years ago a group of researchers conducted a coin box study. The essence of the study revolved around leaving a small amount of change in a public telephone coin return box. As researchers approached people who had discovered the money, they asked if the subject had found any money in the public telephone coin box. About 85 percent of the control group denied finding the money. The second study used the same conditions except that researchers purposely touched the subjects when asking about the money. About 80 percent of the second group admitted to having found the money. The results showed a very high correlation between being touched and admitting to finding the money.

A similar study was done in a library setting, and the results supported the idea that an incidental touch, as a customer was checking out, had a high positive correlation with increased satisfaction scores.

Of course, one must know the difference between incidental touching and sexual harassment.

When the Student Is Ready, the Teacher Arrives

Understanding that people don't care how much you know until they know how much you care is very important, as best explained by the Buddhist proverb "When the student is ready, the teacher arrives." Obviously as a child matures, "when the child is ready, the parent arrives" is equally true. A sense of caring is an essential element in preparing all of us for needed guidance and direction.

Be Tough on Results but Tender on People

Caring does not mean that you do not hold people accountable and require positive results. Nor does it mean that corrective action and feedback cannot be given. In fact, true caring requires accountability and feedback. If you don't provide others with constructive feedback, you are robbing them of the opportunity to improve. Caring comes in when you consider how the accountability and feedback process is handled. Armand Stalnaker was the chairman of General American Life when I first started working there. Early in my career, I heard him tell the leadership team to always "be tough on results but tender on people." That message has stuck with me to this day. It works in all my roles.

Here are some quick guidelines on ineffective and effective feedback:

Ineffective Feedback	Effective Feedback
Attacks the person	Describes the problem
Uses negative labels	Presents positive expectations
Threatens the person	Analyzes the problem
Is punishment oriented	Helps or disciplines
Deals with past	Deals with present or future
Is general	Is specific

Use *I* language rather than *you* language when giving constructive feedback. In feedback situations, *I* language is assertive, as in "I don't understand note 3." Whereas in feedback situations, *you* language is aggressive, as in "You made a mistake on note 3." Also, always be specific. Learning comes from specifics. Only feelings come from generalities.

Attack the Problem, Not the Person

I'm not sure of the origination of this advice, but it is golden. Whenever you find yourself dealing with a negative situation, you will usually have much more success attacking the problem rather than the person. Also remember that *judgments add heat to the conversation whereas descriptions take heat out of the conversation.* Focus on observed behaviors that need correcting, not the person or the person's characteristics. This applies equally in all the roles you play.

Handle People with Care—Summary

Care is a very important part of the BASIC strategy because sometimes the difference between marginal and excellent performance is pretty small, and the level of care can make the difference. In major league baseball, if you get two hits out of every ten at bats, you are a minor leaguer at best. However, less than two more hits in every ten at bats most likely results in election to the Baseball Hall of Fame.

A personal story illustrating the use of care comes from my days as a teenage worker at the Dairy Dell in St. Louis. Mr. Robert Heil was the owner of this Dairy Queen-like operation. I worked for Mr. Heil in the evenings after school. Every night around 8:00 pm, we would get slammed by customers on their lunch break from the evening shift at a nearby factory. In my first week, my job was to fill the milk shake orders while others grilled the hamburgers and fried the french fries. As the orders piled up, I was trying to get the mixer to work faster by turning and shaking the paper cup. Well, I got a little too aggressive, causing the steel mixing blade to split the side of the paper cup, sending chocolate milk shake flying everywhere. As this was happening,  I could feel the cold milk shake hitting me in the face and hands, but for a few seconds, I had no idea what was happening. By the time I figured out what was happening, there was chocolate milk shake all over me, a couple of my coworkers, and the walls of the building. Mr. Heil was not happy, my coworkers were upset, and the customers' orders were delayed as we tried to clean up the mess. I could have been fired on the spot, but Mr. Heil was very tender and attacked the problem, not the person. He recognized how bad I felt about what had happened and even acknowledged that I was trying to do the right thing by speeding up the process. I never forgot how he acted and how caring he was in that situation, and I have since tried to emulate his approach.

Care directly contributes to the overall value of any relationship. Be someone who cares about others and adds value to all your relationships with others. Ask yourself, "Are the others in my life better off because I am here for them, and do they know I truly care?"

For more information on the power of handling people with care, see the book by James Autry titled *Love and Profit: The Act of Caring Leadership*.

Use Your Common Sense

The last and, in many ways, summary element of the BASIC strategy is a *C* for *common sense*.

Following are the key concepts related to using your common sense:

- If all else fails, trust your common sense.
- Listen to your intuition.
- Watch for BFOs.
- Knowledge without common sense is folly.

If All Else Fails, Trust Your Common Sense

François-Marie Arouet (Voltaire), a French Enlightenment writer, historian, and philosopher, said,

> Common sense is not so common.

Some time ago, a Gallup survey of 1,500 people in Marquis's *Who's Who in America* indicated common sense was the number 1 quality most directly accountable for their success. As Ralph Waldo Emerson said,

> People are often astounded by common sense.

Listen to Your Intuition

Don't discount the value and importance of your intuition. Studies have shown that men and women have the same level of intuition, but women have the intelligence to more often listen to their intuition. Don't discount the value of your gut feelings. While I am not proposing actions without thinking, I am suggesting that we can all rely a little more on our own common sense.

Remember the Golden Rule?

- One should treat others as one would like others to treat oneself.

But consider following a modified version of the Golden Rule:

- One should treat others as you think they would want to be treated.

The modification is not to assume the other person's values match your values. If you haven't a clue about their values, then follow the Golden Rule.

Watch for BFOs

BFOs are blinding flashes of the obvious. There is a French and Ethiopian proverb that says, "Fish discover water last," meaning that we often fail to recognize that which is most obvious. In other words, something that is taken for granted. Watch for BFOs. Cary Phillips mentions putting wheels on luggage as a BFO. Why did it take so long for someone to come up with this idea?

Sometimes we make things harder than they really need to be. Read the following:

> Aoccdrnig to rscheearch at Cmabrigde Uinervtisy, it deosn't mttaer in waht oredr the ltteers in a wrod are, the olny iprmoetnt tihng is taht the frist and lsat ltteer be at the rghit pclae. The rset can be a total mses and you can sitll raed it wouthit a porbelm.
>
> Tihs is bcuseae the huamn mnid deos not raed ervey lteter by istlef, but the wrod as a wlohe. Amazing, huh?

Often, if we have the essence of something (like the first and last letters above), we can figure out the rest. I believe using a little common sense and watching for the BFOs can lead us to better relationships.

Knowledge without Common Sense Is Folly

Some very smart people either lack common sense or at least fail to use it. Sometimes we overthink in situations where we should rely more on our feelings. Valuing our feelings is especially true in human interactions. We seem to desire rationality when we know life isn't always rational. Often we lack, or fail to use, our common sense because we allow our general intelligence to override our common sense.

Use Your Common Sense—Summary

As Charley Jarvis once said, "The average person has an enormous reservoir of common sense because they haven't used any of it yet."

Review the summary graphic of the BASIC commonsense ideas included in the front and back of this book.

Final Thoughts

Different from many motivational writers and speakers, I do not have a particularly personal heartwarming story. Fortunately, I have all my senses, was not a prisoner of war, am not a politician, etc., and grew up in a reasonably good environment (maybe poor in dollars, but rich in most other ways). Nor am I a star athlete, a TV meteorologist, a newscaster, or even an unusually successful businessperson or author.

In other words, I am a lot like most readers. Just a commoner, but one who thinks and really knows that we all can do a lot better in all our relationships if we keep these BASIC strategies in mind.

The secret to better relationships is as common as we are. We need to start recalling and using these BASIC strategies.

Remember, what we are aspiring for is progress, not perfection. Implementation of the BASIC strategies is part of the journey, not the destination.

As stated many times throughout this book, the strategies and tools suggested herein are not new or revolutionary. They involve commonsense ideas such as getting to know yourself and others better, thinking before acting (but not ignoring our valid feelings), keeping a balance in our lives, showing care for others, and being better communicators.

When dealing with leadership, partnership, and parenthood—if you can't understand something, go back to the basics, and you'll find some guidance. As Somerset Maugham once said,

The greatest truths are too important to be new.

With apologies to Mr. Maugham for paraphrasing,

The BASIC truths are too important to be new.

Summary of the BASIC Strategy—Page 1

BASIC Relationship and Leadership Strategies

"Real human freedom is the ability to pause between the events of our lives and choose how we will respond." - Rollo May

Understand **B**ehavior and keep your **B**alance

Begin each circumstance **A**new

Be **S**ituational

Watch the "**I**"

Practice **C**ommunication, **C**are and **C**ommon sense

Reaction

vs.

Choice

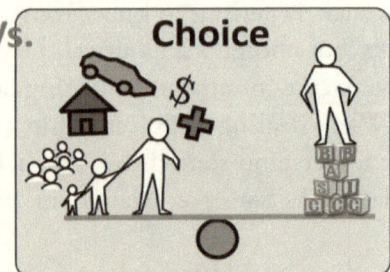

"The greatest truths are too important to be new." -
Somerset Maugham

BASIC Relationship and Leadership Strategies

11100 W. 124th Street • Overland Park, KS 66213
913-707-7079 • www.basicrelationships.com
For more information, email Paul Heacock at pheacock@kc.rr.com

Copyright © Basic Relationships 2014
V 2.0

Summary of the BASIC Strategy—Page 2

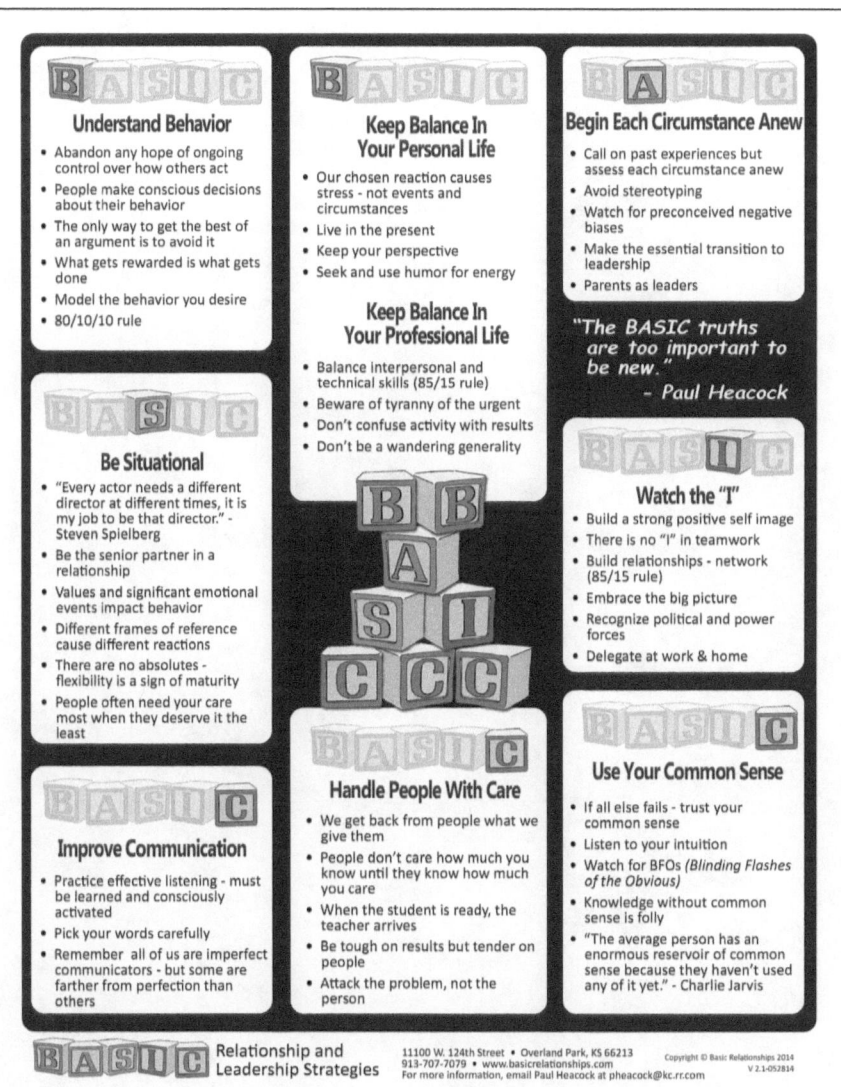

Understand Behavior

- Abandon any hope of ongoing control over how others act
- People make conscious decisions about their behavior
- The only way to get the best of an argument is to avoid it
- What gets rewarded is what gets done
- Model the behavior you desire
- 80/10/10 rule

Be Situational

- "Every actor needs a different director at different times, it is my job to be that director." - Steven Spielberg
- Be the senior partner in a relationship
- Values and significant emotional events impact behavior
- Different frames of reference cause different reactions
- There are no absolutes - flexibility is a sign of maturity
- People often need your care most when they deserve it the least

Improve Communication

- Practice effective listening - must be learned and consciously activated
- Pick your words carefully
- Remember all of us are imperfect communicators - but some are farther from perfection than others

Keep Balance In Your Personal Life

- Our chosen reaction causes stress - not events and circumstances
- Live in the present
- Keep your perspective
- Seek and use humor for energy

Keep Balance In Your Professional Life

- Balance interpersonal and technical skills (85/15 rule)
- Beware of tyranny of the urgent
- Don't confuse activity with results
- Don't be a wandering generality

Handle People With Care

- We get back from people what we give them
- People don't care how much you know until they know how much you care
- When the student is ready, the teacher arrives
- Be tough on results but tender on people
- Attack the problem, not the person

Begin Each Circumstance Anew

- Call on past experiences but assess each circumstance anew
- Avoid stereotyping
- Watch for preconceived negative biases
- Make the essential transition to leadership
- Parents as leaders

> "The BASIC truths are too important to be new."
> – Paul Heacock

Watch the "I"

- Build a strong positive self image
- There is no "I" in teamwork
- Build relationships - network (85/15 rule)
- Embrace the big picture
- Recognize political and power forces
- Delegate at work & home

Use Your Common Sense

- If all else fails - trust your common sense
- Listen to your intuition
- Watch for BFOs (Blinding Flashes of the Obvious)
- Knowledge without common sense is folly
- "The average person has an enormous reservoir of common sense because they haven't used any of it yet." - Charlie Jarvis

BASIC Relationship and Leadership Strategies

11100 W. 124th Street • Overland Park, KS 66213
913-707-7079 • www.basicrelationships.com
For more information, email Paul Heacock at pheacock@kc.rr.com

Copyright © Basic Relationships 2014
V 2.1-052814

About the Author

Paul Heacock lives with his wife, Janis, in Overland Park, Kansas. He retired from full-time work on January 1, 2014, and now offers keynote presentations and facilitates training on financial literacy as well as BASIC leadership and relationship strategies.

www.ingramcontent.com/pod-product-compliance
Lightning Source LLC
Chambersburg PA
CBHW030901180526
45163CB00004B/1660